Marcus Wesson, Vampire King of Fresno

Ruth Kanton

Published by Trellis Publishing, 2021.

While every precaution has been taken in the preparation of this book, the publisher assumes no responsibility for errors or omissions, or for damages resulting from the use of the information contained herein.

MARCUS WESSON, VAMPIRE KING OF FRESNO

First edition. July 8, 2021.

ISBN: 979-8224743919

Written by Ruth Kanton.

MARCUS WESSON, VAMPIRE KING OF FRESNO

RUTH CANTON

Marcus Delon Wesson

Marcus Delon Wesson was born on August 22, 1946, in Kansas City. He was the first born child of Ben and Carrie Wesson, who went on to get three more children after Marcus. The second born, a daughter named Cheryl, was born a year after Marcus, Detri, the second daughter, was born two years later, while the last born, Michael, was four years younger than Marcus. The family moved often, and managed to settle briefly in different cities before they packed up and left again. Most of the relocations were because the family had gotten evicted from their homes. Carrie Wesson was the disciplinarian of the house, as well as the provider for the most part. Ben Wesson was an alcoholic, and his children mainly described him as neglectful and sadistic. He worked odd jobs, but spent most of the money on alcohol. He often got into drunken brawls, and on one occasion, he came home with his throat slit. Carrie was able to convince him to go to hospital, and he was stitched up. His relationship with the children was confusing, as he related to them in ways that crossed the line of appropriate behavior, but none of them ever accused him of molesting them. The children admitted that he was abusive, but offered no details regarding the abuse. Carrie was a devout Seventh Day Adventist, and always ensured that the family was in church every Saturday without fail. She was described as a Christian fanatic. She would pray with the kids every night, attend and host Bible meetings several days in the week, and would create hand-written notes and devotions for her children. The family's dedication to the church remained even with their frequent relocations.

When Marcus was 10, the family moved to San Jose, California. The family quickly joined the Ephesus Seventh Day Adventist church in San Jose, where Marcus joined the church choir and sang bass in a male quartet. He attended Samuel Ayer High School until 12th grade, and while he attended the graduation ceremony, he never actually got his diploma. His life at home was complicated, especially after his grandmother, cousin Larry Morgan and niece Patricia left Alabama and moved in with them. Ben Wesson's relationship with Larry Morgan was suspicious, as the two men seemed too close even for relatives. A few months after Larry moved in, Ben moved out of the family home and cohabited with Larry in a cottage in San Jose. Ben stayed away from his family for ten years, returning to his wife in the late 1970s. His father's bisexuality had a great effect on Marcus, who seemed to embrace the idea of same sex unions instead of rejecting it. By this time, he had concrete ideas about polygamy, bisexuality, and homosexuality, and tried to get others to agree with him on the subjects. He was a bit of a loner, but was mainly categorized as a good guy with quirky ideas. With no high school diploma, Marcus decided to join the U.S. Army when he was 19.

Rose Solorio

On June 2, 1966, 19-year-old Marcus joined the U.S. Army. He trained for 10 weeks as a medical corpsman. For the next two years, Marcus was a specialist 4, Medic in the 695th Medical Ambulance Company. He was deployed to Europe during the Vietnam War, where he drove the Army ambulance. He was honorably discharged in 1968, and he returned to San Jose. He began attending college classes, but quit before getting his undergraduate degree. A few weeks after returning home, he met Rose Solorio, a woman 13 years his senior. The two began dating, and Marcus moved into her home. Rose was separated from her husband, and had several kids already. She was unemployed, and lived on Welfare. In 1971, she gave birth to Marcus' son, Adair. Marcus was 25 at the time. Marcus' relationship with Rose took a strange turn when he set his eye on her 14-year-old daughter, Elizabeth Solorio. Marcus began a sexual relationship with Elizabeth, and strangely enough, got Rose's permission to get married to the teenager. Marcus and Elizabeth got married in 1974, but they decided to keep it a secret from the family. However, this became impossible to do when Elizabeth got pregnant in March 1974.

When he noticed his sister's pregnancy, Jesse, Rose's older son, confronted Marcus about it. In response, Marcus got an electric cord and mercilessly beat up Jesse, who was unable to remove his shirt in the locker room at school so that his teammates wouldn't see the marks. However, family members had begun suspecting that Marcus was abusing the kids, and when they found out about the beating, they called the cops. Marcus knew that he would go to jail if Jesse told police what happened, so he struck a deal with the family. He stated that he would leave the home if Jesse promised not to tell police what happened. However, he had one condition – he would go with the family van. He stated that if they didn't let him have the van, he would leave with his son, Adair. This sparked another fight with Jesse, who picked up a screwdriver and promised to kill Marcus with it. In the end, Marcus left with the van, but left Adair behind. Elizabeth sat in the passenger seat and moved away from home with Marcus. She was 15 at the time, and he was 27.

Elizabeth Solorio

After she got pregnant, Elizabeth dropped out of James Lick High School. She maintained that she needed to be available to take care of the kids. The first born, Dorian Wesson, was born on December 12, 1974, a few months after they left her mom's home. A year later, on November 6, 1975, she gave birth to the second son, Adrian Wesson. It seemed that Marcus was more than ready to start the big family he had always wanted. Marcus took a job at a Wells Fargo Bank as a teller to make ends meet. However, the conservative work environment stifled him, so he quit his job and began growing his dreadlocks. He later swore never to work again in his life.

By 1986, Elizabeth and Marcus had 11 children – Adrian, Dorian, Kiani Wesson (born April 23, 1977), Sebhrenah Wesson (born in 1978), Stefan Wesson (stillborn in 1979), Almae Wesson (born in 1980), Donovan Wesson (born in 1981 and died six months later of spinal meningitis), Marcus Wesson Jr. (born December 2, 1982), Gypsy

Wesson (born December 28, 1983), Serafino Wesson (born February 19, 1985) and Elizabeth (Lise) Wesson (born March, 28, 1985). The children were all homeschooled by Elizabeth, who believed that public schools were "too dangerous" for the children. Once he was out of a job, Marcus went on Welfare to support the family.

Illabelle Lee

In October 1978, Marcus and Elizabeth were at a Seventh Day Adventist Church in Santa Cruz when they met Illabelle Lee, a white pregnant teenager with long blond hair. Illabelle had just gotten off the bus and was planning to attend a service at the church for the first time when she was greeted by the Wessons. Illabelle had run away from home after she got pregnant since it had become the cause of conflict in the home. She was alone, and the friendship she struck with Elizabeth was on a different level. She lived with Marcus and Elizabeth, and would attend church services with them. The three were an odd sight, but they were okay with the arrangement. Illabelle trusted Marcus, and she would confide in him often. Towards the end of 1979, Illabelle's relationship with Marcus became sexual. However, he only permitted oral sex between them, because Elizabeth was not willing to let her bear Marcus' children. While Marcus told Illabelle that he loved her many times, she always felt like she was not at the top of his priorities like Elizabeth was.

Illabelle was the only one in the house who worked, and all her paychecks were turned over to Marcus. She feared that if she refused to turn over her money or accept his sexual advances, he would end the relationship. Marcus told Illabelle that he wouldn't be able to marry her, but offered her the position of being Elizabeth's handmaiden. She ran all the errands for Elizabeth, and anything that was asked of her. However, she began wanting more commitment from Marcus, but this seemed more and more of an impossibility. She realized that Elizabeth was the one controlling the relationship, so she decided to leave. With the help of her brother, who lived out of state, she was able to buy a car. Within a week after getting her driver's license, Illabelle drove away from the Wesson home and never saw them again.

Welfare Fraud Charges

While living in Santa Cruz, Marcus decided to find a boat to convert into a living space for his family. He found one in Marin County owned by a man named Kenneth Nelson and bought it for $14,000. He paid for the boat in monthly $500 installments, using money orders and travelers' checks. The sale was finalized in October 1987, and Marcus was the owner of a twenty-six-foot sailboat. He found a marine surveyor and paid him to sail it from Paradise Key in Marine County to the Santa Cruz harbor. Marcus knew that if the Welfare Department found out about his purchase, he could lose his government benefits. He approached a friend, Stoney Burnett, and asked him to register the boat in his name. In return, Stoney would get 1% of the sale price of the boat when Marcus decided to sell it. However, Marcus had signed the vessel owner's report, and the tax assessor's office discovered this. They called the Welfare Department, and action was taken against Marcus. Stoney initially told investigators that the boat was his, but later admitted that he had never seen it. Santa Cruz County sued Marcus, and a fierce legal battle ensued. Marcus defended the purchase, claiming that the boat was the family's residence. The District Attorney pointed out that the boat could only comfortably accommodate four people, let alone a family of ten. Marcus maintained that his only fault was lying to the department by failing to notify them of the purchase.

Additionally, the welfare investigators discovered that the family was living on a plot of land in the Santa Cruz Mountains. No one was able to verify where Marcus had gotten the $14,000 used to buy the boat. The jury found his guilty of two felonies – welfare fraud and perjury – after only deliberating for a single afternoon. The judge on the case, Judge William Kelsay, sentenced Marcus to three months in jail and five years' probation. He appealed the ruling, but the appellate court upheld the sentence in 1992. After his sentence, Marcus stopped including his name in any official documents – including his children's birth certificates. In addition to his legal problems, Marcus had a feud with the harbor master for failing to pay his docking fees, amounting to $2,300. After Marcus' arrest, the boat was sold and part of the proceeds was used to clear the outstanding debt.

Santa Cruz Mountains

In the 1980s, Marcus bought a piece of land in the remote Santa Cruz Mountains. He also got a prefabricated home, but lost both the home and the house after failing to keep up with the mortgage payments. For the next 10 years, Marcus and his family split their life between the Santa Cruz Mountains and the harbor. In the mountains, Marcus had struck a rent-to-own deal with A.J. Wheeler, the owner of a remote piece of land along Summit Road. He took $500 from the welfare check and paid Wheeler the down payment for the quarter acre piece of land. To avoid losing his government aid, Marcus made Wheeler promise to leave out his name on any documents. Marcus set up a campsite on the land, and they lived there periodically from the late 1980s to the early 1990s. By this time, Elizabeth's sister, Rosemary Solorio, had been having drug problems, and sent her three daughters – Sofina Solorio (from her marriage to Danny Vasquez), Ruby Ortiz, and Brandy Sanchez (from her marriage to Ruben Sanchez) – to live with the Wessons.

In 1995, Marcus moved the family on a more permanent basis to the mountains. During this time, three of the girls – Kiani, Ruby, and Sofina – were pregnant. They were all carrying Marcus' babies. The decision to relocate away from the harbor was partially influenced by the Solorio's family criticism of Marcus' sexual relationship with his daughters and nieces. Jesse was perhaps the most vocal, but no matter what he said to his sister, Elizabeth always stood by Marcus. The family lived in full seclusion in a large army tent, and with no running water, they had to fill gallon jugs on their way to and from Santa Cruz.

Kiani and Sofina known they were pregnant before they moved to the mountains, but Ruby discovered her pregnancy shortly after they moved to the camp. Kiani gave birth to a girl, Illabelle Wesson (named after Illabelle Lee) on September 16, 1995. Six months later, Sofina gave birth to a boy, Jonathan Wesson. Three months after Jonathan was born, Ruby was taken to Watsonville Community Hospital where she gave birth to a girl, Aviv Wesson. Ruby's sister, Brandi, was eight years old when Marcus began sexually abusing her. On one occasion, they were sitting next to each other on the couch, and Brandi had a blanket draped over her lap. Marcus put his hand under the blanket and began penetrating her with his fingers while the other members of the family were in the room. Living in the mountains, 17-year-old Brandi knew that her uncle would get her pregnant next, so she ran away one morning before dawn.

A. J. Wheeler, the owner of the land the Wessons were living on, died in 1997. He left no written proof of the deal that he had made with Marcus, so the Wessons had to vacate the land when Wheeler's son sold it.

The *Sudan*

In the late 1990s, Marcus moved his family to Marshall, California. The remoteness of the town was what he was looking for, and he hoped to keep his family's secrets hidden. He moved the family into a sixty-five-foot retired tugboat called *Sudan*. It was one of the five boats Marcus owned, and none of them were functional. Fifty feet from the *Sudan* was *Raven,* a forty-foot boat the family used to store their clothes. The third boat, known as "The Ark" by locals, was so top heavy that it would have been flipped over by a wave. Marcus had added wood to decorate the boat, which he planned to use to give tours. The plan never materialized. The fourth boat, the *Abejas,* sank after a storm, and *Phoebe,* the fifth boat, broke apart during a storm. Residents of Marshall found the family strange, but they all agreed that the children were quiet and well-behaved. They would row into town in a small boat early in the morning to find supplies. The carried water in gallon jugs, and would dispose toilet waste in the portable toilets on the beach.

Marcus, having vowed never to work again, got the girls jobs at the Marconi Conference Center. Every morning, the girls rowed the boat while Marcus sat at the hull. He then drove them to the center, where they would work 10-hour shifts. Colleagues described the girls as shy and good workers, and were well liked. However, they were not allowed to talk to men, and every week, he would interrogate them about their days. They were encouraged to rat out the others, and were beaten with a small bat if Marcus deemed they had done something wrong. Elizabeth did minimal work around the house, and every chore and childcare fell to the children. Marcus ran a tight ship, and the family almost exclusively lived on beans while he ate meat sometimes. While on the *Sudan,* Marcus' religious inclinations became more pronounced. He believed in Christianity and vampires, and began writing his manuscript detailing his beliefs and personal life. He preached his doctrine to his family, and encouraged them to watch vampire and violent movies. He even explained that they would never be separated, and if anyone tried to do so, they should choose death. While the children did not fully understand what he meant, they knew that death was the only choice if anyone tried to separate them.

The residents of Marshall began finding the Wesson family a nuisance. The children would be seen on the beach, scrounging for food in the trash cans. Some of them complained to the harbor office, explaining that the kids were rummaging through the trash cans, and the older ones were bathing in the public bathrooms, clogging the sinks. Marcus also routinely sent the kids to the upper harbor area to search for aluminum cans. He maintained that he was trying to teach them humility. Residents got concerned that the kids were not attending school. Finally, Child Protective Services was called in, but there was no follow-up visit since the Wessons moved often. One resident, David Harris, was the most inconvenienced by the Wesson family early movements. His house sat on the shore of the Tomales Bay, where Marcus would drag his boat to the shore every morning at 5 a.m. Harris' dogs, woken up by movement in the morning, would begin barking non-stop, waking up Harris. He confronted Marcus several times, asking him to cease his morning activities, or he would put up a fence around his property. Despite the fact that he was the one trespassing, Marcus threatened to sue Harris if he erected the fence. Eventually, Harris got fed up with the Wessons early morning rude awakening, and he called the Marin County Sheriff's Department to report the issue.

The sheriff's office looked into the matter, and when the harbor police inspected the boat, the found various violations. He was ticketed for not having enough life jackets on the boat, and the sheriff's department cited him for illegally living aboard the boat since it failed to meet two requirements of a watercraft residence: A vessel had to move on its own power, and it had to be done every five days. The *Sudan's* engine was non-functional, so in 2003, the Wesson family was ordered to evacuate. The department posted evacuation notices on the four boats – *Phoebe* had already broken up and sank – but the family kept coming and going after that. Following the eviction notice, Marcus moved some of the family members to Fresno. However, Sofina, Kiani, Sebhrenah, and Almae were left aboard the *Sudan* (despite the eviction notice) so that they could keep working at the Marconi Conference Center. He returned several times in a week to pick up their paychecks, and to check if they had enough propane and food. He also kept up his weekly talks with the girls, which included having sex with one of them afterwards.

While living on the *Sudan,* Marcus had three more children. His daughter Sebhrenah gave birth to a boy, Marshey Wesson, on August 8, 2002. His niece, Rosa Solorio, Ruby's other sister, gave birth to Ethan Wesson on July 16, 1999, and to Sedona Wesson on September 9, 2002.

Fresno

Since their eviction from the Santa Cruz Mountains, the Wesson family lived on and off in Fresno and Marshall. Needing to have his whole family together after the Marshall eviction, Marcus began looking for jobs for the women of the family. He secured interviews for Sofina, Ruby, Kiani, and Sebhrenah at a McDonald's on the west-side of town. They were all hired. However, the older boys did not move with the family, and Dorian and Adrian remained in Santa Cruz on their own. However, they had to pay Marcus for their independence by sending him money for two years. The rest of the family moved into a small upstairs section of a duplex on College Avenue. Fresno was less secluded, so the women were able to socialize more at work. Ruby, finally realizing that women can have their own independent lives, decided to run away. However, Marcus was able to draw her back by using her love for her daughter, Aviv. He beat her up for trying to run away for ten days consecutively. She tried again, but was drawn back in again because of her daughter. Sofina's attempt at leaving the family met a more violent consequence – Marcus stabbed her. She survived, but was always looking for a way out.

Marcus moved his family to an apartment on Huntington Avenue, where he decided to purchase a bigger home. Using the money he had saved up from his daughters' and nieces' paychecks, he put down a third of the $100,000 price of a two-story Tudor-style mansion that had been gutted by a fire on 1999. He put the house in the women's name, and made a deal with Frank Muna, a lawyer who sold him the house, to make monthly mortgage payments directly to him. The house was uninhabitable because of the extensive fire damage, so Marcus moved the family into the shed behind the house. Despite their best efforts, the family got behind on their mortgage payments, so Muna sued the women. He also sued them for stealing property worth $15,000 from the shed. They lost the court case, and were ordered to vacate the premises and pay Muna $30,000 to cover the property taken from the garage. In July 2003, they sold the house for $149,500 and used part of the proceeds to pay Muna the money they owed.

By the time the house was sold, Marcus was a father again. His daughter, Kiani, had given birth to her second child with him, Jeva Wesson, on February 22, 2003. However, Ruby and Sofina were able to finally break away from the family. Ruby ran away after she fell in love with a co-worker, and Marcus asked Sofina to leave after she got pregnant with another man's baby, Milton, who she worked with. Milton was old enough to be Sofina's father.

761 West Hammond Avenue

In October 2003, Marcus finalized the purchase of the small, flat-roofed building on 761 West Hammond Avenue. He put the house under Rosa Solorio's name. The building was zoned as a business, and the city served Marcus with a notice to evacuate the premises soon after the family moved in. On March 12, 2004, Elizabeth left the home to visit a family member, and left Marcus and Sebhrenah working on the school bus parked outside the home, which Marcus was restoring, using coffin lids as seats. On the same day, Sofina and Ruby were finally ready to put their plan into action – with the help of brothers, uncles, and cousins from their mother's side, they planned to storm into the West Hammond home and take their children with them. They got to the house that afternoon, and since they knew Marcus' name wasn't on Jonathan's and Aviv's birth certificates, the government would let them keep the kids once they got them out.

When they got to the home, Rosa, Sebhrenah, and Marcus were outside working on the bus. Sofina walked into the house, and found her son Jonathan in the front room. She tried taking him, but her sister, Rosa, began arguing with her. Kiani heard the noise and made her way to the front room seeking to find out what was going on. Outside, Ruby and the others were talking to Marcus when Louis Garcia, Brandi's boyfriend, began recording the conversations going on around him. Inside house, Sofina had pulled Jonathan by the hand to lead him out of the house when Rosa grasped the other arm. After a few moments of tugging, Rosa pried Sofina's hand loose. Sebhrenah walked into the room and pulled Jonathan behind her. Sofina was holding a chair when Marcus walked in and demanded to know what they wanted. He spoke calmly. As Ruby spoke to Marcus, pleading with him to let them take their babies, Sebhrenah made her way into the back bedroom. Sofina followed, and Lise walked behind her holding the hands of 4-year-old Ethan and 7-year-old Aviv. Rosa was holding Jonathan's hand as they walked into the room. Inside the bedroom was 8-year-old Illabelle, 1-year-old Marshey sleeping on the floor, and Jeva in her crib. Sofina tugged on Jonathan's hand again, but Rosa and Sebhrenah took him into the room and shouting began. When Marcus called for her, Sofina went to him, followed by Lise, Sebhrenah, and Rosa. The children were left in the bedroom. Outside, relatives began calling police after they heard shouting from the house. Sebhrenah and Lise walked into the bedroom and closed the door. Sofina pushed it open, and managed to wedge herself halfway into the room when Kiani and Rosa appeared and pulled her out of the room. Inside, Sebhrenah was rummaging through a bag.

Marcus called Sofina again, and she went outside where he was standing. When her mother, Rosemary Solorio showed up, another argument ensued, with Rosemary asking her daughters to leave without the kids. The shouting escalated, and Rosemary attacked her son Danny and punched Ruby in the stomach. Marcus tried to reason with Sofina and Ruby, promising them visiting rights. They wouldn't budge, and maintained they wouldn't leave without their kids. After five frantic calls to 911 by the Solorio relatives, Fresno police officer Frank Nelson finally arrived, with his partner officer Benny Martinez. Martinez moved the family members a few steps away as Nelson talked to Marcus and his two nieces. He asked for Jonathan's and Aviv's birth certificates, which the women provided, along with their IDs. He told Marcus that he would need to file his case with the courts asking for custody.

Marcus wouldn't be reasoned with, so Nelson called in his superior, Sergeant Patrick Jackson. As Jackson explained to Marcus that the courts needed to be involved, Rosemary punched Sofina in the stomach. She was restrained by relatives as more officers arrived at the scene.

Sergeant Jackson tried explaining to Marcus what he needed to do to get custody, but was getting nowhere. He then asked that CPS be called in. When he stepped away to radio in his request, Marcus retrieved a key from a small black pouch and handed it to Rosa, who walked back into the house. After speaking to a lawyer and CPS, Jackson informed Marcus that the kids would be taken by CPS. Officer Nelson stepped in, and asked if there were any other kids in the home, and Marcus said no. Nelson explained that CPS would take all the kids found in the home.

Serafino arrived, and after a short argument with the police, walked into the house and spoke to Kiana and Sebhrenah, who was crying. He assured them that nothing would happen to them or the kids. Outside, Marcus tried to plead with Ruby to come inside and talk, but she refused. Elizabeth arrived and found chaos outside her home. As Sofina spoke to her aunt, Ruby looked up and realized that Marcus was missing. She asked where he had gone, and one uncle stated that he had walked into the house. Sofina, convinced that her uncle had gone to kill the children, desperately ran to one of the officers and pleaded with him to go into the house and check on the kids. Guns drawn, several officers walked to the door, where Serafino was standing guard. They asked him to move, but when he started arguing about warrants, two officers pulled him out of the way. Inside, the officer saw Elizabeth leave the back bedroom crying, and she ran out into the yard. "They're all gone! They're all gone!" she cried and fell into Sofina's hands.

Massacre

The SWAT team was called in, and Fresno officers surrounded the house with guns drawn. A crime scene tape was secured around the home, and family members were asked to take cover behind the yellow school bus. The SWAT team arrived, and officers asked Marcus to step out on the house. At 4:47 p.m., officers watched as a figure emerged from the back bedroom. When he walked out into the light, officers quickly noted that his clothes were covered in blood, and he removed an empty knife sheath from his pocket. Officers entered the dark house, with Officer Eloy Escareno the first to enter the home. Using a flashlight, he made his way into the back bedroom. He saw the coffins leaning against the wall, but his eyesight wasn't used to the dark. Officer Tello followed him into the room, found a light switch, and flipped it on. Escareno fell to his knees and shouted into his radio "Oh my God! We need an ambulance! Code three! Code three!" On the northeast corner of the room, were stacked bodies, with blood pooling on the floor underneath the bodies. Checking for pulses, Escareno found none. They counted seven bodies, but it wasn't until the crime scene investigators arrived that they found two bodies hidden at the bottom of the pile. There were nine bodies stacked.

25-year-old Sebhrenah Wesson was at the top of the pile, shot in the right eye. Under her body was a .22 caliber handgun with one live round of ammunition. It was bagged as evidence. Under Sebhrenah was 17-year-old Lise, shot twice in her right eye. 1-year-old Jeva was under Lise, shot in the right eye. Next was Sedona, the 18-month-old, shot in her right eye. Under Sedona was 18-month-old Marshey, shot in his left eye. 4-year-old Ethan was under Marshey, shot in his right eye. 8-year-old Illabelle was under Ethan, shot in her right eye. The last two victims were the Ruby's and Sofina's children – the ones at the center of the dispute. 7-year-old Jonathan and 7-year-old Aviv were also shot through their right eyes. Tests showed that Lise and Sebhrenah died after the seven younger victims.

Death Row

On March 25, 2004, Marcus pleaded not guilty to nine counts of murder, and what eventually amounted to 14 sex charges, including rape and forcible oral copulation. District Attorney Elizabeth Egan announced that the DA's Office would be seeking the death penalty. The mass murder trial of Marcus Delon Wesson began on March 3, 2005. After three months of testimony, in which all the remaining children and Elizabeth testified, the lawyers provided closing arguments. It was now up to the jury to decide whether Marcus would get the death penalty. After 10 days of deliberation, the jury of five men and seven women reached a unanimous verdict on all twenty three counts. While they found that Marcus hadn't pulled the trigger himself, they sided with the prosecution's argument that he either aided and abetted in the murders, or conspired to commit the murders. He was also found guilty of 14 sex crimes, including rape, forced oral copulation, and continuous sexual abuse. The jury also found that the special circumstances of the multiple murders were true. After the penalty phase of the hearing, which was filled with Marcus' last ditch antics, the jury deliberated for less than nine hours before issuing their verdict – death for each of the nine counts of first-degree murder.

The sentencing hearing was held on July 27, 2005, and the judge allowed family members to address the court before he delivered the verdict. The judge concluded: "Therefore, Marcus Delon Wesson, it is the judgment and sentence of the court that you shall suffer the death penalty. Said penalty to be inflicted within the wall of the state prison of San Quentin, California, in the manner prescribed by law and at a time to be fixed by this court in the warrant of execution."

Marcus Delon Wesson is currently on Death Row at San Quentin State Prison, about thirty miles south of Marshall.

TED BUNDY

KENNETH PUTNAM

Ted Bundy is one of the most prolific serial killers of the 20th century, having kidnapped, raped, and murdered at least 36 attractive young women between 1973 and 1978 in Colorado, Oregon, Utah, Florida, and Washington; however, many assert that this figure could be much higher. He had also kept some of his victims' body parts—including heads—as trophies in a utility shed behind his Utah home, as well having engaged in necrophilia with decomposing corpses which he would groom and apply makeup.

A master manipulator and classic antisocial personality, Bundy escaped custody twice; once from court during his first murder trial and the second time from the Garfield County Jail in Colorado by sawing a hole in his cell ceiling. He was placed on the FBI's Ten Most Wanted list and was later arrested in Florida in February 1978 after stealing a car. He was sentenced to death in 1979 for the murder of two Florida State University sorority sisters, and again in 1980 for another murder.

Very charismatic and handsome, Bundy exploited these characteristics heavily with his young female victims in an effort to earn their sympathy trust. He would often approach potential victims in public places, feigning injury or impersonating an authority figure before overpowering them—usually by hitting them in the head with a crowbar—taking them to secluded locations, and raping and murdering them. Sometimes he would simply break into young women's homes and bludgeon them while they slept.

Bundy was originally incarcerated for aggravated kidnapping and attempted assault in 1975 in Utah; however, his list of homicide victims continued to grow. He escaped from custody twice in Colorado and subsequently committed three more murders before finally being apprehended in Florida in 1978. Ted Bundy was sentenced to death and was executed in the electric chair at Raiford Prison in Starke, Florida, on 24 January 1989.

Early Life

Theodore Robert Bundy—originally Theodore Robert Cowell—was born on 24 November 1946 at the Elizabeth Lund Home for Unwed Mothers in Burlington, Vermont. The social stigma of being a single mother was great at that time so Bundy's mother, Louise Cowell, took her infant son to live with her parents—Samuel and Eleanor—in Philadelphia where young Ted took on the Cowell surname and was told that they were, in fact, his parents and that his mother was his sister. Eventually, Bundy discovered the truth and harbored lifelong resentment toward his mother for lying to him.

Bundy's paternity has never been definitively proven. His birth certificate lists his father as Lloyd Marshall, an Air Force veteran and salesman; however, Louise has claimed that she was "seduced by 'a sailor'" whose name "may have been Jack Worthington" but nobody by that name was ever found in Navy or merchant marines records. Compounding the problem is that Bundy's grandfather, Samuel Cowell, has been rumored to be his biological father; thus making Bundy the product of incest; however, again, there is no evidence of this.

In interviews, Bundy spoke highly of his grandparents, especially expressing a fondness for his grandfather even though other family members described Samuel as a tyrannical bully and bigot who beat his wife and dog, abused his daughters, harmed neighborhood cats, and would sometimes "speak aloud to unseen presences". Bundy's grandmother was timid and obedient and was treated for her depression with electroconvulsive therapy.

Bundy exhibited disturbing behavior from a young age. At the age of three, he was alleged to have surrounded his sleeping aunt, Julia, with household knives—blades pointed toward her—and smiled at her when she had awakened.

In 1950, when Bundy was only four, Louise changed both her and her son's surname to Nelson and moved them both to Tacoma, Washington, to live with cousins Jane and Alan Scott. In 1951, Louise met hospital cook Johnny Culpepper Bundy at a church singles night and they married later that year. Johnny formally adopted young Ted and he adopted the last name of Bundy. Even with efforts to include young Ted in family activities along with his four half-siblings—who he was often left to babysit—he always was distant. Later, Bundy would tell his girlfriend that Johnny wasn't his real dad, wasn't smart enough, and didn't make much money.

Bundy confessed that he "chose to be alone" as an adolescent and neither had any natural inclination to develop any close friendships nor knew what drove people to be friends in the first place. He would later say that he "hit a wall" and his inability to comprehend social behavior stunted his social development, rendering him required to adopt a façade of social activity. He was terribly shy, self-doubting, and uncomfortable in social situations and often teased for being different. Despite this, he was a good student at Woodrow Wilson High School, was active in a local Methodist church, and was even involved with a local Boy Scout troop.

Bundy would also admit—while on death row—that a part of him as a young child was "fascinated by images of sex and violence" and he called this part "the entity". He enjoyed reading crime books and detective magazines, particularly those that contained descriptions of sexual violence and pictures of dead bodies. Later, before his execution, he would admit that pornography was central in shaping who he was.

Throughout high school Bundy loved to ski and was very good at it; however, his pursuit of this hobby was usually accomplished with stolen equipment and forged lift tickets. He was also arrested on at least two occasions on suspicion of auto theft and burglary but when he turned 18 his juvenile record was expunged. Stealing, for Bundy, did not involve any guilt and, in fact, he had a sense of entitlement about the entire thing. He often said that the thrill of taking possession of something he wanted without remorse was exciting. Many speculate that his "taking" of his victims represented this same concept and provided him with the same rush. Compounding the problem was his sense of entitlement and cunning ability to lie about everything which demonstrates a common trait among psychopaths.

Bundy graduated high school in 1965 and was awarded a scholarship by the University of Puget Sound where he started that fall, taking courses in Oriental studies and psychology. After two semesters he transferred to the University of Washington in Seattle.

He obtained employment as a stock boy and bagger at a Safeway store on Queen Anne Hill, in addition to other odd jobs. As part of his psychology curricula, he would work as a night-shift volunteer at Seattle's Suicide Hot Line where he met and worked Ann Rule who would later become among the world's foremost true crime writers and who penned a biography about Bundy—that was also partly autobiographical about her working relationship with him—entitled *The Stranger Beside Me* (1980).

While in college, circa 1968, Bundy began a relationship with fellow student "Stephanie Brooks" (a pseudonym); however, after she graduated in 1968 and prepared to move back home to California she broke up with Bundy due to what she described as his lack of ambition and immaturity. Bundy was heartbroken after this and, interestingly, all of his victims bore some resemblance to Brooks; particularly the fact that Brooks and all of his victims had long dark hair which they wore parted down the middle.

Shortly thereafter, Bundy returned to Burlington—his birthplace—and learned the truth of his parentage. This discovery made him more dominant and focused.

He managed the Seattle office of Nelson Rockefeller's presidential campaign in 1968 and attended the 1968 Republican convention in Miami, Florida. He reenrolled at the University of Washington with a major in psychology. He became popular among his professors as he was an honor student and also began a relationship with Elizabeth Kloepfer in 1969. Kloepfer was a divorced secretary with a young daughter and the two dated for the next six years until he went to prison in 1976.

Bundy graduated in 1972 with a degree in psychology and went to work for the state Republican Party.

In the fall of 1973, Bundy enrolled in the University of Utah Law School but did poorly because of poor attendance and, consequently, dropped out the following spring.

While in California on a business trip in the summer of 1973, Bundy found his ex-girlfriend "Stephanie Brooks" and the change in his look and attitude was appealing to her. Bundy courted Brooks the rest of the year—while still involved with Kloepfer—and proposed to her, only to dump Brooks shortly after the new year, likely in retaliation for her breaking his heart years earlier. The breakup wreaked havoc on Bundy who became obsessed with her and this obsession "would span his lifetime and lead to a series of events that would shock the world".

Mere weeks later, Bundy began his first murderous rampage in Washington; however, many Bundy experts assert that he likely starting killing in his teens. One case involved eight-year-old Ann Marie Burr from Tacoma who disappeared from her home in 1961 when Bundy was 14. Burr's house was on Bundy's newspaper delivery route and her father was positive that he saw Bundy near a construction site ditch on the nearby University of Puget Sound campus the day his daughter vanished. Despite other potentially incriminating circumstantial evidence, Bundy remains merely a suspect due to a lack of consensus by law enforcement personnel as to whether they believe he actually did it or not. Bundy has always denied killing her.

Shortly before his execution, Bundy did, in fact, tell his attorney that his first attempt at kidnapping was in 1969 and his first "actual murder" occurred "sometime in 1972". While he was a suspect in the December 1973 murder of Kathy Devine in Washington, DNA analysis exonerated him and her true murderer was convicted in 2002.

Bundy's earliest identified murders were committed in 1974 when he was 27.

Bundy was a handsome and charismatic guy, particularly to his young female victims and he exploited these characteristics fully. He was also an adept chameleon, able to blend in and feign belonging which increased his threat to the attractive brunette women he targeted as his victims. This charm and his adroitness at lying and manipulation made him extremely dangerous.

Known Murder Victims

Karen Sparks (often referred to as Joni Lenz), 18 (survived)

On 4 January 1974, 18-year-old Karen Sparks/Joni Lenz was found by her roommates when she didn't emerge from her bedroom that morning. They were not prepared for what horrific sights they saw. Sparks had been beaten badly and a bed rod ripped from the bed was "savagely rammed into her vagina". Sparks was transported to the hospital in a coma and suffered damages which continue to plague her.

However, she was one of the lucky few victims to survive an attack by Bundy.

Lynda Ann Healy, 21

A very accomplished and beautiful young woman, 21-year-old Lynda Healy announced ski conditions for all of the western Washington resorts on the radio. A senior at the University of Washington, she came from a good family, loved to sing, and was majoring in psychology. She shared a house with four other young women near the university. On 31 January, Healy and some friends went to a tavern and then home to bed. Her roommate in the next room never heard any sounds emanating from Healy's room that night.

The following morning when she didn't emerge from her bedroom after her alarm clock sounded at its usual 5:30 a.m. to go to work—and her job called looking for her—her roommate noticed that her bed was made in a peculiar way. Further inspection showed that the top sheet and a pillowcase were missing, a small bloodstain that was the same type as Lynda's was on the pillow and the bottom sheet, and a bloody nightgown was hanging in her closet. One of her outfits was missing. Also worrisome was that one of the doors was unlocked.

Initially, due to the absence of fingerprint, hair, or fiber evidence, police did not suspect foul play; however, later, they did come to realize that an intruder came in, removed Healy's nightgown and dressed her in another outfit, made the bed, wrapped her up, and took her out of the house.

Donna Gail Manson, 19

On 12 March, in Olympia, 19-year-old Evergreen State College student Donna Manson was kidnapped and murdered.

Susan Elaine Rancourt, 18

On 17 April, Susan Rancourt, 18, disappeared from the Central Washington State College campus in Ellensburg while walking across campus, alone, at night.

Later, two other female coeds would report meeting a good-looking man with his arm in a cast—one the night Rancourt disappeared and one three nights earlier—who asked for assistance with carrying books to his VW Beetle.

Roberta Kathleen "Kathy" Parks, 22

Kathy Parks, 22, was last seen on 6 May on the Oregon State University campus in Corvallis en route to meeting friends for coffee.

Brenda Carol Ball, 22

22-year-old Brenda Ball was last seen leaving the Flame Tavern in Burien, Oregon on 1 June.

Georgeann Hawkins, 18

In the early morning hours of 11 June, University of Washington student and a member of Kappa Alpha Theta Georgeann Hawkins, 18, left her boyfriend's dormitory en route to her sorority house through an alley. She was never seen again; however, witnesses later stated they had seen a man with a leg cast struggling to carry a briefcase in that area. Another female coed reported that he had asked her for help in carrying his briefcase to his VW Beetle.

Bundy later confessed to having lured Hawkins to his car, clubbed her with a tire iron he had hidden underneath his vehicle, and then took her elsewhere to rape and strangle her to death.

Janice Ann Ott, 23, and Denise Marie Naslund, 19

On 14 July, Janet Ott, 23, and Denise Naslund, 19, were abducted mere hours apart from Lake Sammamish State Park in Issaquah, Washington, in broad daylight. On that day, eight different witnesses reported seeing a handsome young man with his arm in a sling who called himself "Ted" and who asked several women for help unloading a sailboat from his VW Beetle. One witness said she walked with him for a ways but didn't see a sailboat and then declined to help him. Other witnesses stated that they saw the man approach Ott and she was observed walking away with him.

Naslund disappeared four hours later.

At this point, police in King County put up fliers with the suspected murderer's description all over the Seattle area. One of Bundy's psychology professors, former coworker Ann Rule, and Bundy's girlfriend Elizabeth Kloepfer reported him as a possible suspect. In fact, Kloepfer (who since changed her surname to Kendall and penned a book called *The Phantom Prince: My Life with Ted Bundy* in 1981) told the Seattle Police Department that her boyfriend "might be involved" in the recent Seattle murders. She called again later that autumn with more information and agreed to give them recent pictures of Bundy to be shown to witnesses; however, many of them could not positively identify him.

Ott's and Naslund's remains were found on 7 September off Interstate 90 near Issaquah, only one mile from the park where they were abducted. Near the women's remains was an extra femur and vertebrae which Bundy confessed before his execution belonged to Hawkins.

Between 1 March and 3 March 1975, the skulls and jawbones belonging to Healy, Rancourt, Parks, and Ball were found just east of Issaquah on Taylor Mountain. Bundy confessed in his death row interview that he kept the decapitated heads of these four victims in his apartment for some time and that he would revisit this dump site often to engage in sex with the corpses until decomposition became too great to continue. Bundy also admitted that he dumped Manson's body there as well—but burned her skull in his girlfriend's fireplace—however, no trace of her was ever recovered.

Other trophies discovered when Bundy's apartment was searched include photographs of his victims and a large bag of women's clothing.

Nancy Wilcox, 16

Bundy began the University of Utah Law School in the autumn of 1974. On 2 October 1974, 16-year-old Nancy Wilcox disappeared from Holladay, Utah. She was last seen in a VW Beetle.

Melissa Smith, 17

On 18 October, 17-year-old Melissa Smith—the daughter of Midvale, Utah's Police Chief Louis Smith—disappeared after leaving a pizza parlor. Nine days later she was found strangled, raped, and sodomized.

Laura Aime, 17

17-year-old Laura Aime disappeared from a Halloween party in Lehi, Utah. Her naked corpse was found on Thanksgiving Day by hikers near a river in the Wasatch Mountains. She had been beaten about the head and face with a crowbar and was raped and sodomized. The lack of blood at the crime scene indicated that she was likely killed elsewhere and dumped in this location. Police found no other physical evidence.

Carol DaRonch, 18 (survived)

On 8 November, 18-year-old Carol DaRonch was shopping at the Fashion Place Mall in Salt Lake City, Utah, and was approached by a man in the Sears parking lot who claimed to be a police officer named Officer Roseland. He told her that her car had been stolen and that he would take her to the police station to retrieve it. He took her to his VW Beetle and she became suspicious and asked him for identification. He quickly flashed a gold badge and she got in but refused his order to fasten her seat belt. After a short distance, Bundy pulled over and attempted to place handcuffs on DaRonch but only managed one wrist. He also attempted to hit her with a crowbar which she was able to catch before it hit her head. DaRonch fought back, kicking him in the groin, and as the car was speeding away she jumped out of it.

DaRonch flagged down another car and they took her to the police who confirmed there was no Officer Roseland. Police were able to obtain a description of the assailant and his car and a blood sample from DaRonch's coat. Type O; the same as Bundy's.

Debra Kent, 17

Mere hours after losing DaRonch Bundy abducted 17-year-old Debra "Debi" Kent from the parking lot of a school in Bountiful, Utah, as she was leaving a school play. She had told her parents she was going to pick up her brother at the bowling alley and she would be back to pick them up soon but never returned. She didn't even make it to her car which was still in the parking lot. Police found a small handcuff key in the parking lot and when they tried the key in the handcuffs DaRonch was wearing, it was a perfect fit.

A month later a man called the police and told them that he saw a tan VW Beetle speeding away from the high school parking lot the night Kent disappeared.

Shortly before he was to be executed, Bundy confessed that he dumped Kent's body near Fairview, Utah. After an intense search of the area, a human kneecap which was consistent with someone of Kent's age and size was found; however, DNA analysis was not conducted.

Caryn Campbell, 23

Bundy's first murder of 1975 occurred on 12 January. 23-year-old Michigan nurse Caryn Campbell disappeared between her hotel's lounge and her room while on a ski trip with her fiancé, Dr. Raymond Gadowski, and his two children, in Snowmass, Colorado. Frantic Gadowski called the police the next morning but a search proved futile.

Nearly a month later—and only a few short miles from where she went missing—a recreational worker discovered Campbell's nude body near the road. Animal damage to her body made it difficult to determine the exact cause of death; however, there was evidence of repeated, crushing blows to her head by a sharp instrument. Some of the blows were so violent that one of her teeth separated from the gums.

Julie Cunningham, 26

On 15 March, 26-year-old Vail ski instructor Julie Cunningham disappeared on her way to a nearby tavern. Bundy confessed in prison that he used his crutches ploy to approach Cunningham to ask for her help carrying ski boots to his car before he clubbed her with his crowbar, handcuffed her, and took her to a secluded location where strangled her.

Denise Oliverson, 25

25-year-old Denise Oliverson vanished in Grand Junction on 6 April while riding her bicycle to visit her parents.

Lynette Culver, 13

13-year-old Lynette Culver was abducted from her school playground at Alameda Junior High School in Pocatello, Idaho.

Susan Curtis, 15

Once Bundy returned to Utah, 15-year-old Susan Curtis vanished on 28 June while walking alone to the Brigham Young University dormitories during a youth conference she was attending. Bundy confessed to her murder minutes before his execution.

The bodies of Cunningham, Oliverson, Culver, and Curtis have never been found.

First Arrest, Trial, and Escapes

Bundy was first arrested on 16 August 1975 in Salt Lake City for failure to stop his vehicle for police. A search of his car unearthed a crowbar, handcuffs, ski mask, trash bags, an icepick, and other items the officer thought were burglary tools. The always calm and collected Bundy explained reasons why he had the items such as that he used the mask for skiing and had found the handcuffs in a dumpster; however, Detective Jerry Thompson connected Bundy and his Volkswagen to the DaRonch kidnapping and other missing girls and searched his apartment.

The search yielded a brochure of Colorado ski resorts with a checkmark by where Campbell had disappeared. Bundy was brought in for a lineup before DaRonch and other witnesses at the time DaRonch was kidnapped and they all identified him as Officer Roseland, as well as the man lurking about on the night Debbie Kent vanished.

After a week-long trial, Bundy was convicted on 1 March 1976 of kidnapping DaRonch and was sentenced to 15 years in Utah State Prison. Bundy was then extradited to Colorado to stand trial for murder.

He was able to escape custody twice before his eventual final arrest in Florida. The first escape occurred on 7 June 1977, when he was transported from the Garfield County Jail in Glenwood Springs, Colorado, to Pitkin County Courthouse in Aspen for his preliminary hearing. As he was serving as his own attorney, the judge excused him from being handcuffed and shackled. During a recess Bundy asked if he could research his case in the courthouse's law library. Hiding behind a bookcase he jumped from a second-story window, spraining his ankle when he landed. After shedding his suit, he simply walked through the town of Aspen as roadblocks were being erected before hiking southward on Aspen Mountain.

Near its summit he burglarized a cabin and stole clothing, food, and a rifle before heading toward Crested Butte; however, Bundy became lost and ended up wandering aimlessly for two days before breaking into a camping trailer on Maroon Lake where he took more food and a parka. Bundy then walked back toward Aspen and stole a car parked at the Aspen Golf Course. Two police officers noticed him weaving in traffic and pulled over the six-day fugitive. In the car were maps of the mountains around Aspen that the prosecutor was using to demonstrate where victim Caryn Campbell's body was found. As Bundy was his own attorney, he had the right of discovery to this evidence, thus demonstrating that he had planned his escape.

Bundy's second escape occurred on 30 December 1977, after having his motion for a change of venue to Denver accepted but with the venue being Colorado Springs instead; a city that had historically been hostile to murder suspects. He had managed to acquire the jail's floor plan and a hacksaw blade from other inmates, as well as $500 in cash smuggled in over a six-month period by visitors—particularly one Carole Ann Boone. In the evening while other inmates were showering, Bundy sawed a one-foot-square hole in his cell's ceiling—behind the steel bars—and was able to fit through it into the crawlspace above after losing 35 pounds. Prior to his actual escape, Bundy "practiced" and multiple reports of possible movement in the ceiling's crawlspace were, curiously, never investigated.

On the night of his escape, Bundy piled files and books under his covers in his bunk to look like his sleeping body, climbed into the crawlspace, broke through the jail's ceiling which, incidentally, was the chief jailer's apartment who just happened to be out for the evening with his wife. Bundy stole some street clothes and casually sauntered out the front door.

Bundy stole a car and drove east; however, the car broke down on Colorado's Interstate 70. A passing motorist gave him a ride into Vail where he caught a bus to Denver and then took a flight to Chicago, Illinois. From there he took an Amtrak train to Ann Arbor, Michigan.

His escape was discovered over 17 hours after the fact at noon on New Year's Eve.

Lisa Levy, 20, Margaret Bowman, 21, Karen Chandler (survived), Kathy Kleiner Deshields (survived)

On 15 January 1978—after Bundy had escaped from jail in Colorado, he traveled to Tallahassee, Florida, and attacked Chi Omega sorority sisters at Florida State University. At approximately 3:00 a.m. he entered the sorority house where he raped and strangled 20-year-old Lisa Levy to death; bludgeoned 21-year-old Margaret Bowman to death; and also bludgeoned Karen Chandler and Kathy Kleiner—both of whom survived.

The entire rampage took only 30 minutes.

Cheryl Thomas (survived)

That same morning, a mere eight blocks from the Chi Omega sorority house, Bundy attacked Cheryl Thomas in her bed and bludgeoned her with a wooden club, severely injuring her.

Kimberly Leach, 12

On 9 February, Bundy kidnapped 12-year-old Kimberly Leach from her junior high school in Lake City, Florida. Her raped, murdered, and dumped body was found in Suwannee River State Park underneath a small pig shed.

Bundy then stole another VW Beetle and left Tallahassee, traveling west across the Florida panhandle.

Florida Arrest

On 15 February 1978 shortly after 1:00 a.m., Bundy was stopped by Pensacola police officer David Lee who learned that the vehicle was stolen. After a brief scuffle, Lee had subdued and restrained Bundy and then took him to jail. During the transport, Bundy allegedly told Lee that he wished the officer would have killed him. Once his identity was confirmed, Bundy was transported to Tallahassee and charged with the Tallahassee and Lake City murders.

Florida Trials and Convictions

Among the most damning evidence during Bundy's June 1979 Chi Omega murder trial were bite marks found on Lisa Levy's left buttock which matched a plaster cast taken from Bundy's mouth. Additionally, Chi Omega sister Nita Neary was returning home late that night and saw Bundy as he left. She was able to identify him in court.

Bundy was convicted on all counts and sentenced to death.

In 1980, Bundy stood trial for the Kimberly Leach murder. Again, he was convicted, this time based upon fiber evidence and an eyewitness who saw him leading Leach away from the school. Bundy was, again, sentenced to death.

After his sentences he sought a stay of execution or commutation of his death sentences to life imprisonment by having one of his legal advocates contact his victims' families to ask them to ask for mercy in order to find out where their loved ones' remains were. This ploy for more time failed.

Execution

Bundy ultimately met his demise in Raiford Prison's electric chair on 24 January 1989.

Shortly before his widely-publicized execution, Bundy confessed to 36 murders in seven states; however, many believe that the total number is much higher. Also before his execution, Bundy contacted Dr. James Dobson, psychologist and founder of the Christian evangelical organization Focus on the Family, and agreed to a television interview the day before his execution. In it, Bundy described the influence of pornography on his behavior. While not expressly blaming pornography for his behavior, Bundy did say that pornographic materials shaped and molded his behavior and he would gradually need more violent, graphic, and explicit material to achieve the same "high"; not unlike a drug addict. He claimed that while murdering he was "possessed by 'something ... awful and alien'" and the brutal urge was indescribable. He also claimed that alcohol helped remove the initial boundary for him to commit his first murder. Bundy also admitted that although he believed he deserved the death penalty, he didn't want to die.

Even today, Bundy remains a suspect in a number of open homicide cases and is likely responsible for other victims who will never be identified. In 1987 he confided to Keppel that there were some murders that he would "never talk about" because they were committed too close to home, involved victims who were very young, or were too close to family. Said victims include the aforementioned Ann Marie Burr who Bundy repeatedly denied having murdered; however, Keppel noticed that Burr fits all three of Bundy's "no discussion" categories. In 2011, forensic testing of material from the Burr crime scene did not have enough intact DNA sequences to compare to Bundy's.

Additional potential victims include flight attendants Lisa E. Wick and Lonnie Trumbull, both 20, who were bludgeoned with a piece of wood while asleep in their Seattle home on 23 June 1966 that was very near the Safeway store where Bundy worked at the time, and where the victims regularly shopped. Trumbull did not make it and Wick suffered permanent memory loss.

On 30 May 1969 college friends Susan Davis and Elizabeth Perry, both 19, who were on vacation in Atlantic City, New Jersey—just 60 miles south of Philadelphia—were found stabbed to death in the woods three days later.

On 19 July 1971, 24-year-old elementary school teacher and motel maid Rita Curran was murdered in her basement apartment in Burlington, Vermont. She had been bludgeoned, raped, and strangled. The motel where she worked part-time was adjacent to the Elizabeth Lund Home where Bundy was born and certain similarities to his other crime scenes made Bundy a suspect.

21-year-old Joyce LePage was last seen alive on 22 July 1971 on the Washington State University campus. Nine months later her skeleton was found wrapped in military blankets, carpeting, and rope, at the bottom of a Pullman, Washington, ravine.

On 29 June 1973, 17-year-old Rita Lorraine Jolly disappeared from West Linn, Oregon while 24-year-old Vicki Lynn Hollar disappeared from Eugene, Oregon, on 20 August of that same year. Bundy had confessed to two Oregon homicides but did not identify the victims.

Brenda Joy Baker, 14, was last seen hitchhiking near Puyallup, Washington on 27 May 1974 and her body would be discovered a month later in Millersylvania State Park.

19-year-old Wisconsin native Sandra Jean Weaver who had been living in Tooele, Utah, was last seen on 1 July 1974 in Salt Lake City. Her nude body was found the following day in Grand Junction, Colorado.

20-year-old Carol Valenzuela was last seen hitchhiking near Vancouver, Washington, on 2 August 1974 and her remains were found two months later in a shallow grave south of Olympia; along with the remains of another female who was later identified as 17-year-old Martha Morrison who was last seen in Eugene, Oregon, on 1 September 1974. During this time, Bundy drove from Seattle to Salt Lake City and could have conceivably passed through both towns; however, there is no definitive evidence.

Bundy is also a suspect in Melanie Suzanne Cooley's disappearance on 15 April 1975 after leaving Nederland High School in Nederland, Colorado. Her beaten and strangled corpse was discovered on 2 May by road maintenance workers nearby in Coal Creek Canyon. Whereas gas receipts place Bundy in Golden that day—not far from Nederland—the Jefferson County Sheriff's Office has classified her murder as a cold case.

On 1 July 1975, Shelly Kay Robertson, 24, failed to show up for work in Golden, Colorado, and her nude, decomposed corpse was found in August inside of a mine on Berthoud Pass near Winter Park. While gas station receipts place Bundy in the area, there is no direct evidence as to his complicity.

23-year-old Nancy Perry Baird disappeared from the Farmington, Utah, service station where she worked on 4 July 1975. She officially remains a missing person and Bundy has repeatedly denied involvement.

Finally, 17-year-old Debbie Smith was last seen in February 1976 in Salt Lake City before the DaRonch trial. Her body was found near the airport on 1 April 1976.

Aftermath

During the Kimberly Leach trial, Bundy married Carole Ann Boone. He took advantage of an existing Florida statute in which a marriage declaration in court in front of a judge constituted a legal marriage. Thus, Bundy called Boone as a character witness and married her while she was on the witness stand. After numerous conjugal visits, Boone gave birth to a daughter in October 1982. She returned to Washington in 1986 with her daughter after divorcing him and never returned.

Ann Rule described Bundy as "... a sadistic sociopath who took pleasure from another human's pain and the control he had over his victims, to the point of death, and even after." He once referred to himself as "the most cold-hearted son of a bitch you'll ever meet" and one of his defense attorneys, Polly Nelson, said that Bundy "was the very definition of heartless evil." At one point, Bundy said, "We serial killers are your sons, we are your husbands, we are everywhere. And there will be more of your children dead tomorrow."

Bundy contacted Robert Keppel—the detective who helped put him in prison—while on death row to assist him with the "Green River Killer" investigation at the time. With Bundy's assistance, Keppel was able to understand the inner workings of the mind of a serial killer and was, subsequently, able to identify and apprehend Gary Ridgway in November 2001.

Ted Bundy has been the subject of three television movies and one feature film. The two-part film entitled *The Deliberate Stranger* aired on NBC in 1986, starring Mark Harmon as Bundy. *Ted Bundy* (2002) starred Michael Reilly Burke as Bundy and was directed by Matthew Bright. In 2003 the USA Network aired Ann Rule's *The Stranger Beside Me* that starred Billy Campbell as Bundy and Barbara Hershey as Rule. Finally, the A&E network produced an adaptation of detective Robert Keppel's book *The Riverman* in 2004, starring Cary Elwes as Bundy and Bruce Greenwood as Keppel.

THE TRAILSIDE KILLER

JACK BENSTON

David Carpenter ("Trailside Killer")

David Carpenter, also known as the Trailside Killer, stalked, sexually assaulted, and murdered mostly women on hiking trails near San Francisco, California, with a few victims in Santa Cruz, California. Most of his victims were shot in the head, execution-style, while a couple of them were stabbed to death. Carpenter's reign of terror lasted from 1979 into 1981 when he was subsequently arrested, tried, and convicted of death.

One of his victims, Stephen Haertle, survived being shot multiple times by Carpenter—even though his girlfriend Ellen Hansen was killed—and was able to give police a description of his assailant. Additional witness testimony placed a small red foreign car in the area. Carpenter matched the composite drawn from Haertle's description and he also owned a car that matched the description of the one on the scene at the time of Hansen's and Haertle's attack.

Carpenter was convicted in two separate trials; one in Los Angeles and one in San Diego. Both trials were relocated due to defense attorneys' requests for changes of venue.

He was ultimately sentenced to death and is currently on San Quentin's death row. Carpenter is 85 years of age.

Early Life

David Joseph Carpenter was born on 6 May 1930 in San Francisco—a place that would later become his hunting grounds. As a child, he was physically abused and neglected by his alcoholic father while his near-blind mother was overly domineering. By the time he was seven years old, his stutter was so bad that he couldn't function in any social situation. Many experts assert that his stuttering was likely a result of stress, self-perceived inadequacy, and not feeling safe as a child. Consequently he was ridiculed which made him overly reclusive. Instead of therapy he was forced to take ballet and piano lessons.

To relieve his frustrations, Carpenter suffered from a bedwetting problem and also tortured animals; thus fulfilling two of the three prongs of the classic serial killer triad, with the other being a preoccupation with setting fires.

From a young age he also had an insatiable sex drive and would look for opportunities to express this. At the age of 17 Carpenter was incarcerated for molesting two of his young cousins. He served a year in the custody of the California Youth Authority and apparently learned nothing because after his release he was even more predatory; offending until he got married in 1955.

Carpenter worked a number of jobs, including as a cruise ship's purser, a salesman, and a printer.

Carpenter and his wife had three children and Carpenter's demanding libido got to be too much for her. Eventually his wife was not enough to satisfy him. In addition to his violent rages he would prowl around, looking for other women. When his drive became so desperate, he resorted to violence.

By serial killer standards, Carpenter was a late bloomer. His first serious violent offense occurred in 1960 when he was arrested and incarcerated for attempted murder for attacking a woman with a hammer and knife. He had befriended this woman and invited her over to meet his wife and family. One day he picked her up for work but instead of driving her there he drove to a wooded area near the Presidio and then pretended to be lost. At some point he grabbed her, straddled her, and tied her up with a clothesline. He then threatened her with a knife, forcing her to be still and telling her that he had a "funny quirk" that needed to be satisfied. When she resisted he struck her multiple times with a hammer. Her cries for help alerted a nearby military patrol officer who, essentially, saved her life. When commanded to stop, Carpenter shot at the officer and was met with return gunfire which wounded Carpenter. He was then arrested. The victim survived. The victim described his speech to investigators as slow and deliberate, thus suggesting that when Carpenter feels as though he is in charge of a situation and asserting himself then he loses his stutter.

While initially sentenced to 14 years, Carpenter served just nine before being released in 1969. Tired of his sexual demands and temper—and having just given birth to their third child—his wife divorced him. When questioned about what caused the divorce Carpenter's story would change, thus indicating that he learned to tell people what he thought they wanted to hear.

Carpenter was remarried quickly after his release and in less than a year this marriage failed as he was back to his old tricks. He once tried to rape a woman by hitting her car to force her out of it. As she struggled with him he stabbed her but she managed to get back into her car and get help.

At this point there is little doubt that Carpenter wanted to rape again but not return to prison so he was prepared to eliminate any witnesses.

He was rearrested on 3 February 1970, in Modesto, California, on kidnapping and robbery charges. Before being transferred to prison, however, he and four other inmates escaped from the Calaveras County Jail. After recapture by the Federal Bureau of Investigation, Carpenter was incarcerated for seven years on the kidnapping and robbery charges, with two more for violating parole. He served his time and was then paroled in May 1979, without being listed as a sex offender which he should have been. In August of that year he murdered his first of many victims.

Carpenter found a job at a photo print shop in San Francisco after he left prison and by all measures appeared to be on the right path to becoming a productive and law-abiding citizen.

The Crimes

Edda Kane

44-year-old married bank executive Edda Kane disappeared from Mount Tamalpais Park near San Francisco Bay on 19 August 1979, while hiking in the part of the park nicknamed "the Sleeping Lady" to revel in the glorious view of the Golden Gate Bridge. As she enjoyed an athletic lifestyle and could not find someone to accompany her on her hike that day, she decided to go out alone. When she did not return home that day her husband called the police who sent out a search team with dogs in case she had fallen and required assistance.

Kane's vehicle was in the parking lot where she left it but there were no signs of the missing woman.

She was later found off Rock Spring Trail on 20 August 1979, naked and shot to death. Forensic experts surmised that she had been attacked from behind and then shot execution-style with a bullet in the back of the head based upon the position of her body on its knees with her face in the dirt. $10 was missing from her wallet, along with some credit cards. The attacker took her glasses but left her jewelry.

This was the first murder on Mount Tamalpais.

Kane's autopsy demonstrated that she had been shot once in the back of the head with a .44 caliber gun. As she had not been raped, police were dumbfounded as to the motive for the attack. Nobody who knew the victim could think of anyone who would want to do her any harm and the lack of evidence did not permit police to fully investigate her death. After a short time her murder became an unsolved isolated homicide and things returned to normal until the following spring.

Barbara Schwartz

On 7 March 1980, 23-year-old baker Barbara Schwartz had gone hiking in Mount Tamalpais State Park with her dog and had never returned.

She was found on a narrow unpaved trail, stabbed to death in the chest. A witness who had watched the entire crime ran for help and, thus, led the rangers to the crime scene. The witness was hiking in the area when she saw through the trees a thin, athletic man, about 25 years of age approach Schwartz whose dog was barking. She said the assailant "had a hawk nose and dark hair, and he wore hiking boots." The witness then stated that the man and victim struggled for nearly a minute and then he left as Schwartz fell to the ground which was when she left to seek help. Unfortunately, the witness' description of the assailant was "wildly erroneous in every respect" and she, in fact, later admitted this herself. Consequently, investigators were misled, thus delaying the search for the actual culprit.

Other witnesses said they had seen a lone male in his 40s, wearing glasses, and clad in a raincoat despite the fact that it wasn't raining that day. This man was most likely Schwartz's killer.

The bifocals found near Schwartz's body turned out to be prison-issued so investigators began to look at recently-released convicts, particularly those with a record of sex crimes who bore some resemblance to the witness description of the assailant. The San Francisco office of the FBI assisted with the investigation but to no avail.

Interestingly, however, police in another jurisdiction did question a man who claimed to have been wounded in a convenience store attack; however, these officers did not have access to the Marin County all-points bulletin and, therefore, were unable to make a possible connection that this quiet man may have been responsible for Schwartz's murder. The next day the same wounded man visited an optometrist—Schwartz's doctor, in fact—to get a new pair of glasses. The previous day the police had questioned the doctor about Schwartz's prescription; however, he had no knowledge of the eyeglasses found at the scene of the crime. If he had then he might have recognized the "unique prescription" his new patient had.

During Schwartz's autopsy, the pathologist counted 12 separate stab wounds in her chest, likely made with a ten-inch knife. Several days later, some kids found a blood-crusted boning knife near the crime scene which was determined to have been purchased at a large chain grocery store. A television reporter had subsequently handled the knife, thus obliterating any fingerprints which might have been left by the murderer. Forensic evidence suggested that she, too, had been in a kneeling position when she died.

Anne Alderson

On 15 October 1980, 26-year-old former Peace Corps volunteer Anne Alderson entered the park to go for a jog and to demonstrate that the park was, for the most part, safe. Many witnesses saw her and the park's caretaker even remembered her sitting alone in the 5,000-seat amphitheater to watch the sunset. Earlier that day some of the same witnesses reported seeing a lone male around 50 years of age in the park "just standing around."

She was found the next day with a .38 caliber bullet in her head. This crime scene was different from the others in that Alderson was raped, then permitted to get dressed before being murdered. She was found propped, face up, against a rock with her right earring missing. Investigators believed that "her twisted arrangement" indicated that she may have been forced to kneel as well before being shot.

Mark McDermand—A Red Herring

Police thought they had the person responsible for her death when they investigated a double homicide on 16 October 1980, near Mount Tamalpais in Mill Valley. Mark McDermand, 35, and his brother, Edwin, 40, both lived with their mother, Helen, 75. At approximately 8:30 p.m. deputies responded to a call by a concerned friend. After forcing their way into the home, deputies found the body of a man lying in a hallway who was identified as Edwin. He had been shot in the head and chest. In a locked bedroom deputies found the deceased body of Helen, lying on the bed and covered by a blanket. She had a single bullet hole behind her left ear. Eight spent .22 caliber casings were found near the bodies.

Deputies found a small padlocked door that led to the basement. They discovered a note tacked to the inside of the door addressed to "Shitheels" that said that by the time the note and bodies were discovered it would be "way too late" and that the perpetrator would be found either "on the news or on a 'slab'". The note was signed "Mr. Hate."

Inside the room were spent .38 caliber casings, three .22 caliber bullets, and ankle holsters for a pistol and a knife. This smelly basement room had been Mark McDermand's bedroom and became the prime suspect.

The coroner said that the bodies had been dead for three or four days.

A few days later, the local newspaper and the Marin County Sheriff's Department received letters from an individual claiming responsibility for the double homicide and a handwriting expert stated that the same person who wrote the note at the McDermand's house also wrote these letters. In these letters, the writer stated that he would not be captured alive so on 24 October detectives devised a plan to lure him by running an ad directed at him with a phone number that said that if he surrendered he would be treated fairly.

McDermand called the number that evening and said that he was considering surrendering but that "he had some things to do first." He called again two days later with details about the murders; saying that he tried to kill his mother and brother quickly but miscalculated with Edwin, hence the multiple gunshot wounds. He said that he had to "stop Edwin from hurting others" and that he would turn himself in the next day.

When McDermand approached the police he was wearing a belt with a .38 caliber revolver and also had a set of thumb cuffs and three speed loaders. In his vehicle was a 12-gauge shotgun, a .22 caliber pistol, ammunition, a metal box containing several hypodermic syringes, and some insulin as McDermand was diabetic.

He told police that his brother was schizophrenic and had been deteriorating quickly so he borrowed the guns and then prepared to go on the run after the deed was done. McDermand said that he acted out of diminished capacity and that he, too, was schizophrenic and couldn't remember the murders or when he did he told several different stories.

Nevertheless, the jury found McDermand guilty of two counts of first-degree murder and he received the death penalty.

At the end of it all, investigators resolved his potential part in the trailside murders as none of his firearms matched the bullets found in the victims on Mount Tampalpais. That and the fact that the murders continued.

Shauna May

On 27 November 1980 25-year-old Shauna May disappeared from Point Reyes National Seashore Park while hiking. She was supposed to meet friends the following day to do more hiking. They had selected this area because it was several miles north of San Francisco and had not had the dubious distinction of having had a murder occur there recently. When she failed to show up, her friends alerted park officials.

Two days later her body was found by hikers who had seen her foot protruding from a shallow grave. She had been strangled with picture frame wire, shot three times in the head, and shoved into a shallow trench. She had also been raped.

Her body was found in close proximity to Diane O'Connell.

Diane O'Connell

The body of 22-year-old Diane O'Connell was found the same day and near May's body. She had disappeared a month earlier from the same area while hiking with friends as well and her body was rather decomposed. She had been raped, strangled with wire, and shot once in the head.

It was initially believed that the two women perhaps knew each other and were killed at around the same time as another hiker reported hearing four gunshots in that area of the park during the mid-afternoon.

The two women were laying together, face down. Their collective clothing was piled atop a backpack. A pair of underwear was stuffed into O'Connell's mouth. After investigating, it was determined that the two women did not know each other.

Richard Stowers and Cynthia Moreland

As if finding two bodies wasn't bad enough, police also discovered the bodies of 19-year-old Richard Towers and his girlfriend, 18-year-old Cynthia Moreland on the same day as May's and O'Connell's. The couple had been missing since 11 October, having last been seen by friends who they told that they were going to go hiking in the park. In fact, Stowers was in the Coast Guard and was reported as being AWOL.

Both victims had been murdered execution-style with bullets to the head.

An autopsy placed their time of death mere days before Alderson's, thus suggesting that there were two murderers or that a single killer had gone hunting for victims in two different areas. When ballistics determined that the bullet from Alderson's head matched those in both Stowers and Moreland, authorities knew there was just one single deadly predator.

Visitors were told not to go hiking alone; however, being together did not save Stowers and Moreland. Those who typically frequented the parks stayed away or went elsewhere until the murderer was caught.

Needless to say, the media frenzy that ensued wreaked panic throughout the area.

Was David Carpenter the Elusive Zodiac Killer?

Between December 1968 and July 1969 a man shot two couples on two separate occasions in Vallejo, California and then taunted detectives with phone calls claiming responsibility. One of the victims survived and was able to give police a description. Soon thereafter, editors of three San Francisco newspapers each received part of a strange letter also claiming to be from the killer. His message "consisted of a printed cryptogram composed of symbols and signed with a crossed-circle symbol" and all three of the letters had to be put together to decipher it. A local teacher was able to crack the code which stated that the killer enjoyed killing and it was his intention to continue doing so. He signed his letter "the Zodiac."

On 27 September 1969, while 20-year-old Bryan Hartnell and 22-year-old Cecelia Ann Shepard were picnicking at Lake Berryessa, a man in a black executioner's hood approached them. He stabbed Shepard ten times—five in the front and five in the back—and Hartnell six times in the back. He then called the police to report it.

Two weeks later the killer struck again, killing cab driver Paul Stine. The *San Francisco Chronicle* received a letter soon after accompanied by a torn piece of the shirt Stine was wearing at the time of his death. Investigators developed a number of suspects but none checked out. This serial killer was very clever and turned his escapades into multilayered games before he withdraw and maintained a low profile. This was quite disturbing for investigators who never knew when or where he would resurface.

In 1980, former FBI profiler John Douglas—who had been on the Zodiac case since it began—assisted sex crimes expert Special Agent Roy Hazelwood and San Francisco police to help create a profile of the Trailside Killer.

After examining the crime scene data and photos, Douglas concluded that the killer would be a local man who was shy, reclusive, and may have a speech impediment. Douglas also added that the murderer was likely socially awkward, white, intelligent, blue collar, and had spent time incarcerated. He was presumed to choose his victims out of opportunity rather than hunting the same type of victim. His modus operandi (MO) was to approach from behind and overwhelm his victim—"like a spider waiting for a bug to fly into his web." Douglas added that the killer would also have at least two of three specific background indicators common to many serial killers: bedwetting, fire-starting, and cruelty to animals. Finally, Douglas had said while the suspect likely committed rape in his past he had not killed anyone before his current murderous rampage. When questioned about the very specific speech impediment predictor, Douglas said that the secluded killing areas and method of approach indicated some type of shyness and/or shame and he believed it was due to some physical malady that really bothered the killer. Therefore, he attacked in the way he did to compensate for his handicap. While being very detailed, however, police still didn't have any potential suspects.

After Douglas returned to Quantico the Trailside Killer struck again.

Carpenter was ultimately cleared of any involvement with the Zodiac murders through fingerprint and handwriting analysis.

Ellen Hansen

On 29 March 1981, University of California at Davis undergraduate students Ellen Hansen and her boyfriend Stephen Haertle were ambushed in Henry Cowell State Park near Santa Cruz; another town that experienced a spate of murders during the early 1970s committed by Edmund Kemper, John Linley Frazier, and Herbert Mullin—all of whom were safely incarcerated at that time.

Carpenter approached the couple with a pistol in his hand and threatened the pair, insisting that Hansen permit him to rape her. Of course she refused, telling him off. Carpenter then opened fire, shooting Hansen point blank in the head twice and once in the shoulder. The assailant then shot Haertle and left him for dead. Haertle crawled for help despite wounds that ripped through his neck, a hand, and one eye. He proved instrumental in providing police with a partial description of the murderer: near 50, balding, approximately five-foot-ten to six-feet tall and approximately 170 pounds, with crooked yellow teeth, wearing dark glasses as well as a gold jacket with lettering on the back and a baseball cap. Haertle also remembered that the assailant had spoken in "quick, commanding sentences." This description differed considerably from the description of the Marin County killer; however, the MO was the same.

Other hikers reported that they had seen a man matching the description of the gunman in a red, late model, foreign car, running through the park after the gunshots had been fired.

Investigators were also able to lift some good shoeprint impressions to compare to a suspect when they got one.

Authorities released a composite drawing based upon Haertle's and other witness' descriptions in a number of newspapers to both alert people and hopefully get some leads. Four days later a woman called to describe a man she had met 26 years earlier on a cruise to Japan. She said that the purser on the cruise was a young man named David Carpenter who had been bothering her and her daughter with inappropriate behavior. She also recalled that he stuttered.

Presumably reading the paper and staying abreast with detectives' search for the Trailside Killer, Carpenter decided to grow a beard.

He then decided to kill much closer to home, enabling police to catch him.

Heather Scaggs

On 1 May 1981 police caught a break; however, it would come with another victim. On that day, 20-year-old Heather Scaggs disappeared on her way en route to buy a car with help from a coworker, one David Carpenter; they both worked at Econo Quick Print. She had told her boyfriend, Dan Pingle, that Carpenter "made a special point" of asking her to come alone when she came by to get the car and that his friend was selling it and Carpenter was going to help her purchase it. It was Pingle who informed police that she was missing. Luckily Scaggs had left Carpenter's address and phone number with him.

Scaggs' decomposing body was found on 24 May 1981 in Big Basin Redwood State Park, north of San Francisco. Ballistics from recovered bullets proved that she had been murdered with the same pistol used on Haertle and Hansen. She had also been raped and the DNA from the semen inside of her matched Carpenter.

Anna Menjivas

On 16 June 1981 a jaw bone later identified as belonging to Anna Menjivas was found by rock climbers in Castle Rock State Park. She had been missing since 28 December 1980 and was 17 years old at the time of her disappearance. She had worked part-time at the bank where Carpenter was a client and he often struck up conversation with her. Many believed that he only came into the bank to talk to her. Because the cause of death could not be established and there was scant evidence against him, he was not charged for her murder even though authorities were certain that he had killed her. Her name was added to the list of Carpenter's victims to bring his total to ten murders.

Investigation and Arrest

When police went to Carpenter's house to question him, they couldn't help but notice that Carpenter looked quite like the man in the composite sketch and that he had a shiny red Fiat.

Police discovered that Carpenter had not shown up on any released inmates' records where they initially searched due to a technicality: that he had been released by the state of California to serve a federal sentence and, while out on parole, was technically in federal custody. This issue resulted in the delay and subsequent difficulty in identifying him. That he was a habitual sex offender was another important factor not fully documented in his records.

The police department and FBI set up a surveillance van outside the house at 36 Sussex Street in San Francisco where Carpenter lived with his aging parents and also followed him on his errands, especially when he associated with other known criminals. They approached Carpenter who was walking down the street one day with a shopping bag in his hand to apprehend him. Initially confused, Carpenter then asked for a lawyer; at this point he was told that he was under arrest, to which he, strangely, begged, "Please don't hurt me."

Officers executed a search warrant on Carpenters home and car and found books about local hiking trails and over 60 maps. They talked to Carpenter's former fiancée who told them that he claimed that the gold jacket he once owned was stolen around the time of the Hansen murder; thus circumstantially placing him at the scene where Haertle and Hansen were shot. Further, Carpenter's car matched the one described by the surviving victim and several witnesses, he had the same optometrist as another victim, he had the right distinctive type of clothing, he had a record for violent sex offenses, he suffered from explosive rage and tried to change his appearance with different glasses and facial hair, and he matched many descriptions witnesses gave as the man who had been seen in the area of multiple attacks.

Haertle picked Carpenter's mugshot as the man who shot him and killed his girlfriend. Out of seven more witnesses present at a lineup, six picked him out although not all of them were sure. Police also conducted a car lineup with witnesses identifying Carpenter's Fiat.

He was formally charged with Hansen's murder and Haertle's attempted murder. At his arraignment Carpenter stuttered so badly that he had a difficult time answering the judges questions.

Police were never able to recover the .45 caliber gun that was used in several of his murders; however, a .38 caliber gun that Carpenter had sold to another man, who was on trial for robbery and gladly relinquished it to authorities, was later proven to be the firearm used in the last two murders.

Trial and Conviction

Carpenter's defense attorneys requested a change of venue due to the publicity surrounding his ten murders. However, if attorneys had thought it would make a difference they were mistaken. A change of venue would do nothing to eliminate the incriminating evidence police had against Carpenter. In April 1984, his Los Angeles trial began and on 6 July 1984, Carpenter was convicted of the Santa Cruz murders of Heather Scaggs and Ellen Hansen, and the attempted murder of

Stephen Haertle thanks to the damning evidence that his gun was the one responsible for their deaths. A second jury sentenced Carpenter to die in San Quentin's gas chamber based upon three special circumstances that warranted the death penalty: that he had committed multiple murders; that he had murdered during commission of rape; and that he had lain in wait for his victims. Judge Dion Morrow told the court that, "The defendant's entire life has been a continuous expression of violence and force almost beyond exception. I must conclude with the prosecution that if ever there was a case appropriate for the death penalty, this is it."

Carpenter's second trial began on 5 January 1988 in San Diego. On 10 May 1988, a San Diego jury found Carpenter guilty for five murders. Carpenter was also found guilty of two counts of rape and one count of attempted rape. This trial was different in that Carpenter himself took the stand in his own behalf. He was on the stand for seven days.

Marin County District Attorney Jerry Herman announced that he wouldn't file any charges against Carpenter for Kane's and Schwartz's murders due to inadequate evidence.

In 1994, potential juror misconduct in the second trial was brought to light in that the jury forewoman had known about Carpenter's convictions in Los Angeles for the Santa Cruz murders and had concealed this fact during voir dire for the Marin County trial. Carpenter was not retried as he had already been sentenced to death for other murders. On 6 March 1995 the California Supreme Court refused to give Carpenter a new trial. Justice Armand Arabian said that it was virtually impossible to keep secrets in cases such as this and that he believed that the juror's knowledge had not unduly biased the jury.

In 1997, the California Supreme Court upheld Carpenter's death sentence for the Scaggs and Hansen murders and on 29 November 199 they upheld Carpenter's death penalty from his second trial, with six of the seven justices agreeing that he had a fair trial for the five Marin County murders and had, in fact, been sentenced properly.

In December 2009, San Francisco police reexamined evidence from the 21 October 1979 murder of Mary Frances Bennett. Bennett was 23 years old at the time she was killed. She had been jogging near the Palace of the Legion of Honor in Land's End Park in San Francisco when she was ambushed and stabbed to death. Police reported that she had been stabbed at least 25 times in her chest, neck, and back. Her "butchered" corpse was found under a thin layer of dirt and leaves. In February 2010 San Francisco police confirmed that DNA collected from that murder was sent to the Department of Justice and was subsequently matched to Carpenter.

He remains a suspect in the murders of Edna Kane and Barbara Schwartz.

Aftermath

Some have speculated that Carpenter wasn't technically a serial killer but a serial rapist who killed his victims to eliminate witnesses so as not to return to prison.

Carpenter's case provided the background for Joyce Maynard's 2013 novel, *After Her*.

A series of geocaching caches have been placed throughout Mount Tamalpais in commemoration of Carpenter's victims.

THE TOY BOX KILLER

54

TERRY CAINE

David Parker Ray was a suspected American serial killer and known torturer and serial rapist of women; suspected because no bodies were ever found. However, he was accused by his accomplices of murdering a number of women and law enforcement officials estimate that he is responsible for as many as 60 deaths in and near Truth or Consequences, New Mexico. Ray purchased and refitted a trailer into what he called his "toy box" which was replete with a number of sex toys and torture items for his victims. He also played a very disturbing audiotape for all of his victims explaining what they will be enduring at his hand. Ray was finally arrested after one of his victims managed to escape after three days of torture. Ray stood trial for kidnapping and sexual torture and was sentenced to 224 years in prison; however, he suffered a fatal heart attack while incarcerated at Lea County Correctional Facility in Hobbs, New Mexico, on 28 May 2002.

Early Life

David Parker Ray was born on 6 November 1939, in Belen, New Mexico. He was named David after his uncle David who was accidentally shot in the heart at the age of 13 by his 15-year-old brother Alden just one year earlier. Ray's grandmother believed him to be a reincarnation of her dead son.

Ray's father, Cecil, was an alcoholic and was very abusive to both Ray and his sister Peggy—who was one year his junior—as well as their mother, Nettie. When Ray was ten years old his father left his mother and moved to Albuquerque. They were divorced soon thereafter. When Nettie decided to stay with her own parents, Ray and Peggy were shipped off to their paternal grandparents, Ethan and Dolly Ray. In the six years Ray and Peggy lived with their grandparents they saw their father twice and their mother only a handful of times. Consequently, there were no maternal bonds between Nettie and her children. In fact, Ray said that he didn't get much affection or attention at all during his childhood.

Ethan was a strict disciplinarian who insisted on the utmost standards of dress and behavior and, as such, the children were required to do ranch chores both before and after school and even though the Rays were not very well off, Ethan made sure his grandchildren were clean and presentable. He was also a devout fundamentalist Christian and made sure to instill within his grandchildren his religious beliefs. Any nonadherence to his rules resulted in physical punishment.

Ray attended Mountainair High School in Mountainair, New Mexico, where he was often bullied for his awkwardness and shyness, especially around girls. Ray commented that he didn't have his first date until he was 18 years old. He was also tormented for being soft-spoken and for having to keep his shirt buttoned all the way to the top—per his grandfather's instructions—when all of the other boys had a few top buttons undone. Ray was also a poor student.

Neighbor Audie Miranda always tried to look out for Ray. He would tell the bullies to leave him alone and stated that even though Ray could defend himself, he remained docile, not liking or believing in violence which was ironic considering what Ray would become. The two became close friends and spent a lot of time together on the Ray ranch riding horses, playing cowboys and Indians, and playing desert hide-and-seek.

Ray always had a love of the outdoors.

Miranda would later say that he believed that Ray's ultra-strict upbringing took a toll on his friend. Miranda even commented that he, himself, was scared of Ethan.

Dolly was not much better. Ray said that he hated her and that she "didn't have a clue."

At the age of 12, Ray began building and setting off bombs and other explosives he fashioned in the woods behind his grandparents' house. He said he blew up a lot of tree stumps as a child.

When Ray was 13 his grandparents gave him a Cushman Pacemaker motor scooter. He discovered within himself a natural aptitude for mechanics and delighted in taking it apart and then reassembling it. The once shy and timid Ray became more confident, especially when his classmates who used to torment him needed his services to fix their scooters.

Some accounts state that Ray began to use and abuse alcohol and drugs while in high school. It was also around this time he began to fantasize about raping, torturing, and murdering women. He said that the few times his father would come visit them, he would bring true detective magazines which Ray enjoyed reading. He began having his fantasies which always involved broken bottles. His sister stumbled upon Ray's sadomasochistic drawings as well as erotic photographs of acts of bondage.

At the age of 15 Ray fashioned his own little dungeon under a large piñon pine tree with a hangman's noose and a collection of broken beer bottles he "planned to use on girls someday." He also admitted to digging a hole and engaging in intercourse with the ground when he was lonesome.

After high school, Ray worked as an auto mechanic.

He married in 1959, joking that he was practically a virgin at that time, and joined the United States Army a year later where he was sent to Korea. The Rays had a son in 1960 and Ray had to return home on emergency leave because his wife was leaving the baby alone when she went out to party. He filed for divorce and sought sole custody. His mother, Opel, and stepfather, Cecil, raised Ray's son until Ray was honorably discharged from the military.

Ray married a second time in 1962 when he was 22 years old and a mere 90 days later he went back to court and filed for divorce again because they just didn't "click".

In 1966, Ray married a third time; to a woman named Glenda Burdine. They were married 15 years and had a daughter named Glenda Jean—who would go by "Jesse"—in 1969. Jesse remembered her father as being gone quite a bit, having worked for the railroad, and of having an unusual fetish for padded leather straps and other bondage fare. She said that kids were naturally curious and while they knew about it, it was not a topic to be discussed.

In sum, Ray married four times, was divorced four times, and had two children.

Ray met Cindy Lea Hendy in 1997 when he was 57; she was 20 years his junior. Originally from Washington, Hendy and her boyfriend John Youngblood moved to Truth or Consequences, New Mexico, on the run from the law for grand theft, forgery, and drug offenses, leaving her three children behind. As she had already served time in jail, she was not keen on returning.

The Crimes

The "Toy Box"

Ray spent over $100,000 on his homemade torture chamber he called his "toy box" that he constructed inside of an old white 15-feet-by-25-feet cargo trailer on his Elephant Butte, New Mexico, property. Elephant Butte is a resort town of approximately 2,000 residents, located along an 18-mile-long, 36,000-acre reservoir.

The trailer was stocked with what he referred to as his "friends": bully whips, pulleys, leather straps, metal clamps, bars which spread the victim's legs, surgical knifes and saws which he used to torture women. Inside this trailer were also numerous sex toys, syringes, detailed diagrams that showed different methods for inflicting pain and torture, and a homemade electrical generator. Ray also mounted a mirror on the ceiling above the gynecologist table upon which he strapped his victims because he wanted them to see everything that was done to them.

He also played a recorded audiotape of himself for his victims whenever they regained consciousness. It began with:

*"Hello there, b*tch. Are you comfortable right now? I doubt it. Wrists and ankles chained. Gagged. Probably blind folded. You are disoriented*

*and scared, too, I would imagine. Perfectly normal, under the circumstances. For a little while, at least, you need to get your sh*t together and listen to this tape. It is very relevant to your situation. I'm going to tell you, in detail, why you have been kidnapped, what's going to happen to you and how long you'll be here. I don't know the details of your capture, because this tape is being created July 23rd, 1993, as a general advisory tape for future female captives. The information I'm going to give you is based on my experience dealing with captives over a period of several years. If, at a future date, there are any major changes in our procedures, the tape will be upgraded. Now, you are obviously here against your will, totally helpless, don't know where you're at, don't know what's gonna happen to you. You're very scared or very pissed off. I'm sure that you've already tried to get your wrists and ankles loose, and know you can't. Now you're just waiting to see what's gonna happen next."*

The rest of the tape involves Ray setting forth his "rules" and "procedures" by telling his victims everything—in graphic detail—that would be done to them to include being raped and sodomized by Ray and his friends, engaging in bestiality, being shocked with electricity, and being poked and prodded with a multitude of surgical instruments and sex toys; essentially, being their sex slave to do with whatever they want. The actual recording is widely available online, quite long, and not for the faint of heart as it is extremely explicit.

In the audiotape Ray describes himself as a "dungeon master" who was affiliated with the Church of Satan and that his slaves were for members of his "congregation."

There was also a videotape showing Ray and his girlfriend Cindy Lea Hendy performing such acts of torture upon a female victim who screamed the entire time.

Psychological torture was also important to Ray. He would blindfold his victims, subject them to brainwashing, use fear tactics, and occasional small favors to keep them "off balance".

Many experts classify Ray as a sexual sadist who finds excitement and pleasure from inflicting pain upon a nonconsensual, submissive and inducing them into altered states of consciousness such as when they pass out from the pain. Such a predilection often forms during adolescence; however, experts do not know exactly what causes one to become a sexual sadist.

Ray had multiple accomplices during this time; including, allegedly, several of his girlfriends, particularly his latest girlfriend, Hendy.

During the investigation Hendy allegedly had told a friend—while she was under the influence of alcohol—that she had willingly participated in Ray's attacks because of the adrenaline rush she got from them. She allegedly confided to this person that "there were four to six people who had been killed, dismembered, and tossed into Elephant Butte Lake." While the friend did not initially believe her, after Ray and Hendy were arrested and the details of the crimes were released, he gave statements to police and the media.

Marie Parker

On 5 July 1997, 22-year-old Marie Parker and her two daughters—ages four and five—were evicted from their apartment for non-payment of rent. They were living in a pup tent on the western shore of Elephant Butte Lake at a campsite called Hot Springs Cove; just north of Ray's trailer. In fact, she had borrowed the tent from him and when her campsite became too messy for the fastidious Ray, he had something to say about it.

Parker was a methamphetamine and cocaine junkie and her main supplier was Ray's daughter Jesse. Ray abducted Parker and took her to his toy box where he raped and tortured her for three days after which he gave Yancy a rope and told him that they "were finished" with her. He then told Yancy to kill her which Yancy admitted to doing. They buried the body in a remote area and Ray threatened Yancy's life if he ever told anyone.

Later, when police took Yancy to the area where Parker's body was allegedly dumped, they could not find any evidence. Yancy stated that Ray probably moved the body.

Police found Parker's abandoned car in the parking lot of the Blue Waters Saloon.

Cynthia Vigil

Cynthia Vigil had been working as a prostitute along Central Avenue (Highway 66) at around 10:00 a.m. when her pimp introduced her to Ray and Hendy in a red recreational vehicle. Ray offered Vigil $20 for oral sex and when she entered the vehicle, Ray produced a police badge and told Vigil that she was under arrest for solicitation. Ray and Hendy handcuffed, gagged, and chained Vigil to a fixture inside of the camper. After a few minutes he pulled the vehicle over and then proceeded to cut off all of her clothing, put a metal dog collar around her neck, place her in shackles, and then slipped a leather mask over her head with no eye openings and a zipper for the mouth. She was also told if she resisted she would be shocked.

When they reached Ray's house, after driving for an hour, Vigil said that she was chained to a bed and was made to listen to Ray's infamous five-minute audiotape before being forced to have sex with both Ray and Hendy. Next, Vigil said that Ray put gravy "up" her and had his German shepherd lick it off. Vigil then had her knees attached to a bar, forcing her legs open and was then "measured" with dildoes that had markings on them before having her breasts and genitals shocked with a portable generator. The entire time Hendy had a gun pointed at her.

The next morning, Vigil was taken at gunpoint to the bathroom to relieve herself and then taken back to the bed, fresh and clean white sheets atop it, where her mouth and eyes were duct taped and she was hog-tied with an elaborate collection of interconnected leather straps. A rope was then attached to a pulley from the ceiling and Vigil's entire body was lifted three feet into the air.

The duct tape was ripped from her eyes and she saw her horrified face staring back at her from a video monitor. She said that Ray tied her legs open and proceeded to whip her with a leather belt, whips, and a cat-o' nine tails. Vigil said that the beating excited Ray who then violated her with a "horrendous looking dildo" and took pictures of her suspended body with the toys inside of her.

Later that day he attached an elaborate system of clamps and pulleys to her breasts and genitalia and proceeded to shock her. Her convulsions caused the pulleys to exert force on the clamps. After taking the excruciating pain for as long as she could, she lost consciousness.

For the next two days Vigil was subjected to sexual torture until she was able to escape.

On 22 March 1999, Cynthia Vigil escaped after being abducted by Ray and enduring a three-day torture ordeal. She was able to escape one morning after Ray had left for work and Hendy had left the keys on a nearby table when the latter went into another room to talk on the phone. Vigil—chained to the wall in the den—managed to use her legs and feet to pull the table toward her and get the keys; however, Hendy noticed her efforts and a fight ensued. Vigil was able to free herself while Hendy beat her and even after being hit in the head with a lamp, Vigil managed to stab Hendy in the back of the neck with an icepick she found on the floor. When Hendy fell to the ground, Vigil escaped the house naked save for an iron slave collar and padlocked chains, and began to run down Bass Road in Elephant Butte. Since she had just been taken three days ago, Vigil had not been taken out to the toy box yet.

Vigil was spotted by a couple of passing motorists who did not know what to make of the woman and didn't stop. Vigil finally surprised a woman at home in her trailer watching television who called the police for her. Vigil was then taken to the Sierra Vista

County Hospital emergency room where the chains were cut off and her battered body was cared for.

When police went to Ray's home, they found bloodied sheets in one bedroom with a broken lamp and broken window, thus corroborating Vigil's claims. A pulley device with hooks and chains was mounted on the ceiling and there was a long, coffin-like box along the side of the bed. Large sex toys were on the dresser.

Arrest and Investigation

After Vigil's escape, Ray and Hendy were arrested off Springfield Road in his red Toyota camper. They claimed that they had kidnapped Vigil in an effort to break her of her heroin addiction. Ray and Hendy were taken to nearby Truth or Consequences—formerly Hot Springs—New Mexico and housed in the Cooper Police Training Center.

Both Ray and Hendy were charged with 12 counts consisting of aggravated kidnapping, conspiracy, and aggravated battery and held on $1 million bail.

Soon after Ray was arrested, New Mexico State Police took the case over from the Truth or Consequences Police Department and Agent Wesley LaCuesta—a five-year veteran of the Criminal Assault and Violent Crimes Division—was called on to assist in the investigation. He left his Las Cruces office and headed north to Truth or Consequences.

LaCuesta interviewed Vigil at the hospital. He observed many small cuts on her extremities, injuries to her breasts, welts on her back, and evidence of her being handcuffed.

By early April 1999, over 100 New Mexico State Police and FBI agents were all over Ray's property looking for human remains.

Eleven days after his arrest, Patty Rust committed suicide after assisting law enforcement personnel with detailed drawings of the toy box over the course of four days. Prosecutor Jim Yontz wondered why the FBI would send a woman into a torture chamber where many women had likely been frightened to death by Ray and the torture he inflicted upon them. He then went to visit the toy box. Inside he found a ghastly collection of sex toys, medical devices, whips, clamps, chains, pulleys, rods, saws, and other items for bondage and sadomasochism; in addition to detailed drawings of how Ray liked to torture his victims, medical books on the female anatomy, and, perhaps most damning, a videotape dating back to 1993 showing a woman being tortured.

There was also a television monitor in the right corner of the toy box so Ray's victims could see what he was doing to them if they looked at the monitor while they were secured to the table. He also had a video camera focused upon the table recording everything he was doing. Photographs of the torture he had inflicted upon prior victims decorated the walls, as well as a bunch of dolls which were "strung up in various states of bondage and torture." In addition to the medical texts, Ray had a copy of Brett Easton Ellis' *American Psycho*; a novel detailing violent assaults inflicted by a man when he needed to release steam from his high-stress life that was also made into a film starring Christian Bale. The novel contains very disturbing descriptions of torture. It was presumed that Ray compared himself to the "protagonist" in the novel as he saw himself as in control and his victims as "expendable pawns in his game", even going so far as to call his victims "packages."

With respect to the videotape depicting the torture of one of Ray's victims, the police were able to find the woman on the tape: Kelly Garrett, who had been married mere days before being abducted by Ray and Hendy. Garrett had been held hostage, raped, and tortured for three days before being drugged and left on the side of the road not far from her in-laws' house. Believing Garrett had been out on a drug binge, she was asked to leave and subsequently moved back to Colorado. Investigators found her in Colorado and she stated that she had amnesia for a long time, only recently—as in the past year—remembering what Ray and Hendy had done to her.

The publicity surrounding the case prompted another victim to come forward with her story. Angelica Montano recounted her ordeal at Ray's hands just one month ago.

Angelica Montano

Montano said that she was a casual acquaintance of both Ray and Hendy and had gone to their house on 17 February 1999, looking to borrow cake mix. She said that Ray left the room and then returned with a knife and told her that she was being kidnapped. When Montano looked over at Hendy, she saw the woman holding a gun, pointed at her. She knew they were serious.

Montano said that the couple grabbed, bound, and stripped her before strapping her to a bed and placing a metal collar on her. She said they then attached electrodes to her breasts and shocked her multiple times in addition to "abus[ing] her with various sexual implements." She then said that Ray forced her to give him oral sex.

After having been chained naked to the bed for three days and being subjected to sexual abuse, it was time for Montano to visit the toy box. Ray removed her handcuffs and led her to the bathroom with a long metal leash attached to the dog collar. He bathed her "like a dog, with a chain and everything" Montano would later say. When she was clean, Hendy applied makeup to her face and then draped a robe over her captive's shoulders before Ray and Hendy led her out into the trailer.

In the smaller trailer—the toy box—Montano was strapped to a gynecologist table where she was subjected to additional electric shocks to her genitalia as well as other instances of sexual assault. She said that she repeatedly begged Ray and Hendy to release her and on the fourth day they relented. She was drugged and taken miles away from Ray's property and dumped on a local highway in the desert where a police officer found her.

Even though Montano did, in fact, report the incident to the police, there had been no follow up. When she saw that Ray and Hendy had been arrested, Montano contacted the police again.

Accomplices

In addition to Hendy, investigators discovered two other accomplices: Ray's daughter Glenda Jean "Jesse" Ray; and Dennis Roy Yancy. Yancy and Hendy had dated in the past.

Yancy admitted to strangling Marie Parker—a former girlfriend—after Ray kidnapped and tortured her. Ray videotaped the murder. Yancy also confessed to seeing photographs of one of Ray's ex-wives in various bondage positions as well as watching Ray torture a woman inside the toy box but that he thought it was consensual. Yancy was subsequently convicted of second-degree murder and conspiracy to commit first-degree murder. He received two 15-year sentences. Jesse was also tried and convicted of kidnapping for sexual torture. She was sentenced to seven years and served three, the rest of the time she was on parole.

Hendy was charged with 25 felonies and was looking at 197 years in prison. To save herself, she agreed to plead no contest and testify against Ray and Yancy in exchange for five felony counts and a 36-year sentence. In the Seventh District Court of New Mexico Hendy pled guilty to two counts of first-degree kidnapping for Vigil and Montano, two counts of sexual penetration (rape) in the second degree for the two women, and one count of conspiracy to commit second-degree kidnapping.

Over 100 FBI agents were sent to search Ray's property but they were unable to identify any human remains. Several bones were located but they proved to be of animal origin. Collecting evidence from Ray's home and toy box proved daunting due to the sheer number of items he had amassed for his tortuous pleasure. In one interview, New Mexico Public Safety Director Darren White told reporters that the evidence inside the toy box was "very disturbing stuff" and "literally made my stomach turn."

It was later discovered that Ray would drug his victims with sodium pentothal and phenobarbital to induce amnesia to prevent them from being able to report what had happened to them when they were released. In Kelly Garrett's case, she was unsure about her own recollections of the torture and accompanying nightmares; that is, until the FBI contacted her and, soon thereafter, she was able to remember—in vivid detail—what Ray did to her so she could testify against him in court.

In his recording, Ray described his whole philosophy about drugging his victims and why getting an accurate body count of those victims he killed is impossible. Ray said:

*"If I killed every b*tch that we kidnapped, there'd be bodies strung all over the country. And besides, I don't like killin' a girl, unless it is absolutely necessary. So I've devised a safe, alternate method of disposal. I had plenty of b*tches to practice on over the years, so I've pretty well got it down pat. And I enjoy doin' it. I get off on mind games. After we get completely through with you, you're gonna be drugged up real heavy, with a combination of Sodium Pentothal and Phenobarbital. They are both hypnotic drugs that will make you extremely susceptible to hypnosis, autohypnosis and hypnotic suggestion. You're gonna be kept drugged a couple of days, while I play with your mind. By the time I get through brainwashing you, you're not gonna remember a fu*kin' thing about this little adventure. You won't remember this place, us, or what has happened to you. There won't be any DNA evidence, because you'll be bathed, and both holes between your legs will be thoroughly flushed out. You'll be dressed, sedated, and turned loose on some country road, bruised, heh, sore all over, but nothing that won't heal up in a week or two. The thought of being brainwashed may not be appealing to you, but we been doin' it a long time and it works. And it's the lesser of two evils. I'm sure that you would prefer that, in lieu of being strangled or having your throat cut."*

One can only imagine the pure horror coursing through his victims' minds as they lay, chained atop his torture table, hearing—in very graphic detail—about what they will be enduring.

Trials and Convictions

The press jumped all over the case and soon discovered that everyone who seemingly knew Ray said that he seemed like a "regular" guy. He did not have any criminal record, nor were there any reports about potentially suspicious activities on his property which he leased from the park service. However, reports from the police indicated that he was considerably worse and darker than he initially seemed.

State District Judge Neil Mertz decided that Ray would undergo three separate trials: for Cynthia Vigil, for Angelica Montano, and for Kelly Garrett. The Vigil trial was set to start on 28 March 2000, in Tierra Amarilla. Judge Mertz suppressed Ray's early interviews with the New Mexico State Police and FBI and also banned the media from the voir dire. Just after jury selection, Ray allegedly suffered a heart attack and was taken to a hospital in Las Cruces. The judge postponed the trial for another week and then there were additional delays and several FBI expert witnesses were excluded.

Then, unexpectedly, Judge Mertz decided to start Garrett's trial for her 1996 kidnapping and torture even though it was the weakest case, evidence-wise. Nevertheless, Judge Mertz scheduled it for the end of May. Of course, Ray was pleased with the delays, not to mention Judge Mertz's exclusion of Ray's printed sheet of procedures for handling his slaves as well as all devices found in the trailer for Garrett's trial since nobody could prove they were there in 1996. This left the prosecution with the videotape and the victim's testimony.

When Vigil's trial was actually conducted, it ended in a mistrial because some jurors were not convinced that the women were completely held against their will and there was a subsequent retrial that resulted in convictions for all 12 counts with which Ray was charged.

Montano's trial was delayed indefinitely because, unfortunately, she was rushed to an Albuquerque hospital on 7 May 2001 with pneumonia where she died an hour later from heart failure. She was only 28 years old. As she was one of only three living, known witnesses who were going to testify against Ray, Montano's death dealt a huge blow to the prosecution. However, prosecutor Jim Yontz was prepared to try Ray for Montano's kidnapping and torture by utilizing videotaped statements she had made at a preliminary hearing on 15 and 16 April 1999.

When prosecutors started "closing in" on his daughter Jesse who assisted with some of Ray's earlier kidnappings, Ray decided to take a plea bargain. He received a sentence of 224 years in prison.

Ray suffered a fatal heart attack while incarcerated at Lea County Correctional Facility in Hobbs, New Mexico, on 28 May 2002.

Aftermath

Yancy was paroled in 2010 after serving 11 years of his sentence; however, his release was delayed because of difficulties stemming from his parole plan which had to be established before release. Three months after he was released in 2011, he was charged with violating his parole and subsequently returned to prison and required to serve his entire sentence until 2021.

Ray is suspected of murdering his one-time business partner, Billy Bowers. The two men bought, restored, and sold cars. On 22 September 1988, Bowers disappeared and his family immediately offered a $5,000 reward for any information leading to his safe return. On 28 September 1989, a fisherman found a male body floating in McCrea Canyon which is along the eastern shore of Elephant Butte Lake. The body was wrapped in a blue tarp and secured to two heavy boat anchors. It had a single bullet hole to the head and $49.47 in a pocket but no identification. There were no missing persons reports for a five-foot-ten-inch male in his late-30's or early-40's so the John Doe remained unidentified for over a decade until Cindy Hendy told police that Ray had murdered Bowers. Hendy admitted that Ray confessed the murder to her and told her that since then he had learned to open the victims' stomachs so they would "stay down" when submerged in water and not float to the surface as was the case with Bowers.

When the body was exhumed and dental records compared, the John Doe was, in fact, Bowers. His son Michael was able to retrieve the body of his long-lost father for a proper burial and some closure.

In November 2002, state police officially opened the toy box to the public in the hopes that renewed media attention might help identify additional victims. Inside were signs that said "Satan's Den" and "Bondage Room." The obstetrical table was still there with all of its clamps, leg stretchers, electric wires, chains, and straps. A steel cabinet held numerous surgical instruments and the coffin-shaped box used to terrorize and contain victims was nearby. Ray's meticulous records detailing what he did to his victims was also available. To ensure that none of his victims escaped, Ray had devised an elaborate alarm system and had written instructions to ensure that all straps were secure prior to leaving the toy box.

However, with Ray dead, the investigation went cold, especially since no bodies were ever found, no possible victims were identified, and no suspicious deaths which might have been loosely linked to Ray were solved. Despite the lack of any dead bodies, he is oft-labeled in numerous sources of literature as a serial killer.

According to Jim Fielder in his 2003 book *Slow Death*, both Vigil and Garrett went on to form relationships and start families of their own.

As recently as 2012, additional evidence has been uncovered which indicated there may be additional victims.

CLASSIFIED AD

RAPIST

71

VICTORIA MANN

Criminal psychologist and behavioral scientist often find themselves debating on the effects of nature versus nurture when dealing with people who cause harm to others. The argument stems from the possible theories of a person's physiology and biology affects or is affected by the environment in which they are raised. For serial killer and rapist Bobby Joe Long, both nature and nurture shaped who he became later in life. Long was born with medical issues that would plague him later in life. His medical situations would increase as he experienced one after another after another accidents and incidents leaving him with damage to his head and physical facial deformities. These physiological issues would then be compounded by a broken household with an unconventional parenting, a life riddled with early exposure to sexuality, drugs and alcohol, and abuse. As Long passed through the years, his reactions to the world around him and his treatment of people would escalate until he would spend almost two years raping, beating, and murdering a string of women before the law finally stepped in an put in behind bars.

Bobby Joe Long was born on October 14, 1953 in Kenova, West Virginia to Joe and Louella Long. Long was born with Klinefelter Syndrome, meaning he had 47 instead of 46 chromosomes, one extra X chromosome. This medical diagnosis would be an early, but overlooked, warning sign about Long's development both physically and mentally. With the extra X chromosome, males often see delayed puberty, growth of breast tissue, smaller testes, and hormonal imbalances. With a starting point already giving Long problems that would affect him psychologically and medically, the young boy had an unfortunate beginning. Klinefelter Syndrome also causes delayed and slower learning abilities, language development barriers, and usually a more introverted and emotional social reaction to people and the situations around them.

Joe and Louella Long divorced in 1955. Joe stayed in West Virginia while Louella Long took Bobby Joe and moved to Miami, Florida. This would be the beginning of a back and forth living pattern for Long, and where his issues with his mother would start to blossom. Later it was established that Long was often left with the landlord while his mom was out for long amounts of time. It is not clear whether she was always working, or if this is when her reputation for being out with different men had started. Though only two years old, Long would look back as this being when his mother began habits that would later color their relationship.

In the summer of 1957, Long had the first of many accidents that would cause further damage to him physically and result in mental repercussions. That summer Long was pulled under the waves at the beach by the strong undertow. Long nearly drowned and would make the comment later in interviews that his mother was "too busy looking at other men" to be paying attention to him and preventing the incident. A year later, in 1958, Long fell off of a swing while playing. He received the first of many concussions and ended up having a stick puncture his eyelid. His mother took him back to West Virginia and began seeing his father again. Though his mother and father would have an on and off again relationship, they always returned back to Florida in less than a few months or weeks. By fall of 1959, Long was beginning first grade in Miami, though he failed to pass and would repeat first grade the next year. During 1959, Long had another accident. While riding his bike he hit a parked car, throwing him over the vehicle. Several of his teeth were knocked out and Long ended up with another concussion. The following year would be spent going back and forth between Miami, FL and Kenova, West Virginia while his parents tried to re-establish a relationship. He completed first grade in West Virginia.

1961 was a rather rough year for Bobby Joe Long. During the spring he was hit by a car. His face was directly impacted by the front bumper knocking him unconscious and ending with him hospitalized in West Virginia. In the fall, Long ran out into traffic and was hit by an oncoming car. Once again he would have more teeth knocked out, but this time he would be left with a deformed jaw from the accident. At another point during the years of 1960-1961, Long was riding a pony when he fell off. Though he was not hospitalized, the resulting head injury left him dizzy and nauseous for quite some time afterwards. In 1962 Long once again found himself returning to the hospital. This time was from a fall from a fence that caused a laceration on the left side of his head, resulting in stitches. Bobby Joe Long already had the misfortune to be born with a brain altering health issue, having a drowning incident and having six head injuries in less than five years would cause a build-up of scar tissue in his brain that wouldn't be noticed until he had a psychiatric evaluation after his arrest. Ironic, as Long spent the majority of his jobs as an X-Ray technician in varying hospitals.

By 1963, Joe and Louella Long decided to end their marriage again. Louella Long took Bobby Joe and moved back to Florida. This time they would live in a house with several of her family members. So many family members lived in the home that Bobby Joe Long was forced to share a bed with his mother. His home situation in combination with his deformed jaw made fourth grade a difficult time for Long. He was repeatedly bullied and made fun of by his peers. Long's mother began working two jobs, one as a waitress and another as a bartender. When she wasn't working she was usually with a different man. Between her job and social life, she began dressing in revealing and provocative clothing. Long began taking out a lot of his aggression on his mother. He verbally began abusing her, often referring to her clothing and lifestyle as being "slutty." Long felt neglected, as well, due to his mother's absences and time spent with the other men.

Louella Long bought a new home in Hialeah, FL in 1965 for herself and her son to live in. The parade of different men seemed to not only continue, but escalate in Long's opinion. Long began skipping school and becoming more socially withdrawn and more verbally abusive towards his mother. In 1966 Long killed the family dog. His reasoning was that his mother care more for the dog than she cared for him. He once stated that "she fed the dog fillet mignon and I only got hamburger." Long now had a separate room from his mother and began detaching himself from her. He met Cynthia at this time, the girl that became his best friend and confidant. Long also began developing breast tissue, gynecomastia, a side effect of the Klineflter Syndrome, and had to have them surgically removed. Despite developmental setbacks, he had consensual sex for the first time in 1967 with Cynthia.

Bobby Joe Long committed his first crime in 1968. He and one of his friends stole a car. The charges were dropped, though, and Long was never punished for the act. In 1970 he was arrested for the first time for minor theft. Later that year he began working for Arc Electric on a part time basis. Long dropped out of tenth grade twice but would re-enroll the following year. At this point, Long's abuse towards his mother started to become physical. The next year, 1971, he was accused of rape. The charges were dropped and the victim was assumed to be lying would insufficient evidence was found to corroborate her story. Shortly after starting school again, Long was expelled. His view of women was already shaded by his mother and what he experienced in dealing with her lifestyle, and now his feeling towards authority were also colored darkly, causing more disturbing thoughts and feelings for Long to deal with when his mind was already suffering from multiple destabilizing factors.

Long enlisted in the army in 1972 with hopes of becoming an assistant electrician. After finishing basic training, he was stationed at Homestead Air Force Base in Homestead, FL. Despite having the army to help give Long a better direction in life, his inability to stay away from criminal activity persisted. In one day he received seven vehicle related tickets. Though he did have many small setbacks, Long was able to eventually get his GED with the army. Throughout his hardships, his relationship with Cynthia grew. They were married in January of 1974 in the chapel on base. Unfortunately, despite his luck seeming to improve, Long was in a severe motorcycle accident in February. Long ended up spending several months in the hospital suffering from another head injury, damage to his shoulder, and extensive damage to his leg. Doctor's contemplated amputation but concluded the leg would be able to heal enough that it would not be necessary. After enduring one head injury after another since he was a child, Long began to show more obvious signs of brain damage. His sexual libido began to increase, to an extent in which the nurses notating him masturbating over five times a day while still hospitalized. He also began demanding more sex of his wife, Cynthia.

Due to the damage to his body and the possible brain injuries, Bobby Joe Long was medically discharged from the army in August of 1974, after serving less than two years. Long and his wife moved off base into a trailer, where they would raise their newborn baby boy. Since he was recovering from the accident and now unemployed, Long had ample time on his hands. He began using newspaper ads to look for women to satisfy his new sexual appetite. Long did begin to attend Broward Community College in order to try to complete his electrician training he was hoping to accomplish while in the army. Long was once again trying to bring some semblance of balance back into his life, but now the build-up of what he had lost, his inability to handle emotions well, and the behavioral issues brought on by his brain damage, Long began taking out his aggression on his wife. He was arrested for domestic battery against Cynthia.

Despite their growing problems, in 1975 Bobby Joe and Cynthia welcomed a new baby girl into their family. They move to Ft. Lauderdale in an attempt to find work and spend the next several months moving around and looking for jobs, even in West Virginia. Towards the end of 1976, Long's parents help them buy a house in Hollywood, FL. Long returned to community college and was finally able to become a certified electrician in 1977 and even receive his associate's degree as an x-ray technician in 1978. In November of the following year he got a job at Parkway Medical in Miami as an x-ray tech. His success was once again short lived as 1980 rolled around. In June, Cynthia filed for a divorce. She listed the marital issues as abuse and financial instability. Long moved into an apartment in Ft. Lauderdale alone. Shortly after, his bad luck continued as he lost his x-ray technician job. Long then moved in with a friend, Susan Replogle, in order to have someone to split rent with. The stay was short before he moved again, this time with a friend named Ted Gensel. Susan Replogle, then, moved in with the two men.

1981 brought with it, even more problems for Bobby Joe Long. Susan Replogle reported Long for rape. The charges never held, though, due to insufficient evidence, again. Two weeks afterwards, Replogle was beaten and thrown down the stairs by Long. Around this same time, Long began picking up and raping prostitutes. In October, Susan Replogle filed an assault and battery charge against Long. One month later, Long was charged for sending obscene material to a 12 year old girl in Tampa, FL. Phone records and mailing envelopes left Long with no choice but to plead no contest.

Long spent the majority of 1982 traveling and looking for work. During the first half of the year he went to California to get a commercial driving license through a commercial driving school. He then returned and tried to find work as a truck driver. Eventually he ended up back in West Virginia, living with his parents. Both of his parents stated that he spent most of his time there sitting around and not actually looking for work. It wasn't until February of 1983 that he finally got employment as another x-ray tech at Huntington Veterans Administrative Hospital in West Virginia. Though his fellow employees were quoted saying he was "polite" and "a good worker," Long was fired in April for making his female patience undress when it was not medically necessary for them to do so. In June, Long bought a 1979 2-door maroon Dodge Magnum and moved back down to Florida.

In the Tampa area, Long was once again hired as an x-ray tech. This time he worked at Humana Hospital on a temporary basis. In August he met Elise at the hospital. Long began dating Elise, and due to her devout religious nature, even began attending church with her. Long seemed to be trying to put his life back together again and even sent $4000 in back child-support to his ex-wife Cynthia. Long's past, though, caught up with him. In September, Long was giben a guilty verdict on the assault and battery charge against Susan Replogle. Bobby Joe Long was furious at the conviction and wrote several letters to the judge and the charge was changed to neutral pending further evidence. In November, Long was given his sentence to his no contest plea in the exposure of obscenities to the 12 year old girl. He spent two days in jail and was put on probation. In the early part of 1984, Long was officially acquitted of assault against Susan Replogle. Long was still able to continue a relationship with Elise throughout this time.

On March 6th, 1984, Bobby Joe Long committed his first pre-meditated rape through his habit of browsing newspaper ads. Long responded to an ad for a house that was being sold. He arrived at the Port Richie home with materials to tie up the woman who was showing the house. When the tour of the home reached the bedroom, Long pulled a gun and tied her up, raped her, and then stole her jewelry. This would become Long's source of income as he repeated the tactic numerous times and even quite his hospital job to continue his criminal career. His girlfriend, Elise, never questioned where he got the money or the jewelry from.

It was on March 27th, 1984, that Long's new habit would go to the next level and become his first murder. Long picked up Artis Wick in Tampa as she trolled the streets. She was found strangled a while later. Long claimed she had not satisfied him and he got angry and strangled her. In April, Long abducted Mary Hicks and forced her at gunpoint to drive him in her Jaguar. Mary crashed the car, escaped, and went to the police. Long was later charged for damages and only received probation. Though he was getting by on his thefts, Long got a job in May at Gulf Bay Electric in Tampa as an electrician. A new crime spree was formed, though, and Long was no longer satisfied by just raping and stealing from his victims.

May 4th, 1984 was when 20 year old Ngeun Thi Long (no relation to Bobby Joe Long) was offered a ride home by Bobby Joe Long. Ngeun had recently quit her job as a stripper and was walking the streets at the unfortunate time when Long was prowling for his next victim. Long took her to a wooded area. His MO was established during this murder as he made her strip naked, lie face down on the seat, he tied her hands behind her back, and then raped her. Long then took her out of the car and beat her repeatedly before strangling her with left over rope. Her body was found nine days later, face down, naked, hands still tied behind her back, and her legs spread wide. The rope was still around her neck.

Bobby Joe Long was once again fired on May 23rd. Women he worked with and those that came into contact with him stated that he was rude and overtly perverted in his nature. Other employees stated he was obsessed with porn and his work station was plastered with pornographic material. Long would begin a steady of pattern of committing rapes and thefts on women he found in the classified ads on a near daily basis and raping and murdering women he came across on the streets as often as several times a month.

Michelle Simens' body was found on May 27th, 1984. The 22 year old was a cocaine addict and prostitute that Long picked up on Kennedy Boulevard and taken to the local "lover's lane." Long proceeded with Michelle as he did with Ngeun, making her strip down, lie face down on the seat, tied her hands and raped her from behind. Michelle Simens fought back, though, as Long tried to strangle her with a rope. In his frustration and anger, Long pulled a knife and stabbed her numerous times and finished by slitting her throat several more. Her body was found with the rope still around her neck. Her clothing was tossed into the nearby trees. Investigators would get several pieces of evidence from her murder scene, though. Among these were red fibers, human hair, bare footprints, tire tracks, and semen.

June 8, 1984 was when Long found his next victim, 22 year old Elizabeth Loudenback. Her body was found in an orange grove in Brandon, FL. Long had maintained his MO with the abduction and rape of Elizabeth. This time he sodomized her as well. He then forced her to redress and get back in the vehicle. According to Long, she wouldn't stop crying and saying that she was hurting and so he strangled her. She had her debit card and a piece of paper containing her PIN in her wallet. Long used these to make multiple withdraws from her account throughout the night. Her body was discovered on June 24th, badly decomposed and weighing less than 25 pounds. She was fully clothed and still had the rope Long strangled her with around her neck.

Bobby Joe Long spent June 14th with his children in an overnight stay. By the end of the month he was able to get a job at Tampa General Hospital as a x-ray technician. In July he was finally sentenced for his abduction of Mary Hicks. Long was charged $1,500 in damages and three years of probation. Long moved into a new apartment, but once again his luck would not last. In September he was fired from Tampa General Hospital for failing to get the advanced certification he needed to maintain his job as an x-ray technician. He had already built up a bad reputation with female colleagues and patients for his perverted nature. He did meet another woman, Ruth Allende, who he began dating and had a normal sex life with. Unbeknownst to her, Long was a rapist and murder with few signs of changing his habits any time soon.

Chanel Devon Williams was an 18 year old Long picked up on September 30th, 1984. Long proceeded as he had done before in forcing her to undress, placed her face down on the front seat, and raped her. He beat her and attempted to strangle her but Chanel was extremely athletic. Long once again lost his temper, this time he pulled a gun and shot Chanel Williams in the back of the head. Long tossed her body under a fence and threw her clothing out of his window as he drove away, causing it to get caught along the fence and the sign for the ranch he had taken her to. Her body was found on October 7th while Long was raping and killing Kimberly Hopps, another 22 year old. Five days later, Long repeated the pattern with Karen Beth Drinsfield. Her body was found in an orange grove a day later on October 14th. Another woman, Vicky Elliot, also went missing during this time period. Two weeks before Kimberely Hopps body was found, Long was once again spending the night with his ex-wife and children. Shortly after his visit, Long would take another woman, but this time would be very different.

On November 3rd, 1984, Bobby Joe Long kidnapped 17 year old Lisa McVey. Long forced McVey into his car at gunpoint and made her perform oral sex on him as he drove her back to his apartment, something he had not previously done. Once at his home, Long raped McVey, but seemed to quickly regret what he did. According to McVey, Long showered her and referred to her as his girlfriend. He started telling her how pretty she was and trying to say nice things while being delicate with her. Long did try to sodomize McVey, but stopped when she said it hurt too much. Long brushed her hair and clothed her and even made her a sandwich and had her eat. Long's gun was on the nightstand, but he unloaded it stating that he did not want to do anything stupid or to be tempted to use it. Long then blind folded McVey and took her back to his car. He gave her a description of a random black man and told her to say that guy was the one that had taken her. Due to the blindfold being loose, McVey was able to see the car and the landmarks around them while they drove. Long reached a parking lot and helped McVey out of the car, kissed her goodbye and left. McVey ran home and made it there by 4:30am. She woke her father and told him what all had happened. Her father immediately went to the police.

On November 6th, 1984, the skeletal remains of Virginia Johnson were found. The police at first believed that she had been dismembered, but further analysis showed the skeleton had been torn apart by scavenger animals. Four days later, on November 10th, 21 year old Kimberley Swann was driving erratically; she had a history of driving under the influence of drugs and alcohol. Bobby Joe Long coaxed her to pull her car over to the side of the road. Long offered Kimberley a ride and she got into his car. The two ended up arguing, and Long became furious with the woman. He strangled her and pushed her body out of the car onto the side of the road. Her body was found two days later. The body of Vicky Elliot was found on November 16th.

Police got a break on November 15th, 1984. Bobby Joe Long was pulled over when his vehicle matched the one police were looking for. Due to lack of immediate evidence, police took a photograph of Long and his vehicle and released him under surveillance. The next day, the same day

Vicky's body was found, police got a warrant for Long's arrest listing his crimes as abduction, kidnapping, and involuntary sexual battery in the case opened for Lisa McVey. Bobby Joe Long began confessing almost immediately. On November 18th, 1984, Long was charged with eight counts of murder and sexual battery, nine counts of kidnapping, and violating his parole. Three days later Artis Wicks body was found. On November 28th the judge ruled the case needed to be seen in front of the grand jury. On December 5th, 1984, Long was charged with the murder of Virginia Johnson.

Bobby Joe Long was held in prison while the courts sorted through the plethora of murders and rapes to build a case against him. On June 18, 1985, a private investigator gave police a suicide letter, confessing his crimes, that Long had written. Bobby Joe Long was moved into the infirmary for close observation and to protect him from self-harm. A psychiatric evaluation was given to Long in February. The doctor's conclusions were consistent with the brain injuries Long had received over the years, along with mental illnesses that he inherited from his parents and that resulted from the Klinefelter Syndrome. Bobby Joe Long was a sexual sadist with bipolar and manic depressive psychosis. The scar tissue and constant damage to his brain over the years had caused organic personality syndrome and temporal lobe epilepsy that caused him to go into altered states of consciousness. The doctor explained that these lapses were usually what occurred when Long would go into bouts of anger and begin beating, or in some cases stabbing and even killing, women.

The Klinefelter Syndrome already left Long with hormonal issues that caused him to have over reactions and overemotional feelings in different situations. The bipolar disorder was believed to have been inherited from his mother. Long then had the repetitive accidents and occurrences of damage to his head causing constant tears and swelling that then would scar over, building up the tissue and resulting in more problems. With Long's mother having the on and off again relationships with his father, the questionable taste in men, clothing, and work and their relationship souring as it did, Long built a very negative view of women. His anger then became more sexually oriented and resulted in his sprees of rape and murder. Long often felt disgusted by women and degraded them when he could, making them little more than a sexual item to him.

As the year carried on, and despite the psychological evaluation and results, Bobby Joe Long was charged in the various crimes he had committed, from the abductions to the rape and thefts to the rape and murders. Each sentence being more stern than the last. When Long had confessed, he had asked for a lawyer and one had not been given to him. Though he did confess that same day, this would cause issue in the first trial. The first major trial was for eight of the murders and Lisa McVey's kidnapping, abduction, and rape. On September 24, 1985, Long agreed to a plea bargain and plead guilty to all. He received 26 life sentences total and would not have any possibility of parole. He also received seven life sentences that, after the first 25 years, he could attempt to appeal for parole. Though his confession was thrown out, the evidence in the case clearly matched Long's vehicle to the red fibers and witness reports and the semen and prints to Long himself. In 1986, the Michelle Simms trial began in Tampa, Florida. The evidence allowed the district attorney to ask for the death penalty and it was granted. Several more cases began to arise and were sub sequentially tried and Long was convicted. Long did appeal the first degree murder and death penalty verdict for Virginia Johnson. The case went forward to an acquittal and became stagnant.

Currently, Bobby Joe Long is on Florida's death row. Despite several attempts at appeals, acquittals of some of the random rape cases because of lack of evidence, the majority of Long's sentencing equates to over several thousand years behind bars and is capped with the death penalty. The fiber analysis came under fire in the nineties when it was discovered that one of the lab technicians was not following protocol. Although Long and his defense team tried to utilize this to his advantage, the plethora of other incriminating evidence along with witness testimony and his confessions made little difference in the effect of the fiber analysis in the case results. It was unfortunate that Bobby Joe Long seemed to be cursed at birth. Being born with an extra x chromosome, his Klinefelter Syndrome caused him psychological issues from his hormonal and emotional imbalances very early in life. Suffering from multiple head injuries and then deforming facial injuries, Long had a very difficult time socially interacting with people. He found himself being pulled back and forth between Florida and West Virginia with his parents' constantly changing marital situation. He then had the difficulty of living with a parent that was gone a lot, saw different men constantly, and living in difficult households, including one in which he would share a bed with his mother as he began the early years of puberty. Long did have chances at redemption. He met Cynthia, the first person he ever confided in, his first love, his first wife, and the mother of his children. He seemed to keep contact with her, long after their divorce, and even tried to stay current with child support and visiting his children. Even though he went on to have several other normal relationships and even good jobs, Long would sabotage each one and always fall back to his habit of using newspaper classifieds to take advantage of women. When rape and theft wasn't enough, Long then began his abduction, rape and murder of women he found on the streets. Bobby Joe Long had a very difficult life and it is hard to say whether he would have led a different life if not for the Klinefelter Syndrome and multiple injuries as a child. Could he have had a normal childhood and became a normal functioning adult? Or was the damage and hormonal issues just an added fuel to the raging fire that burned within him? Psychologists still debate the issues of nature versus nurture and how much that weighs in on criminals like Bobby Joe Long. The only definitive information is that he will never again have the chance to try to be a different person, but he will also never again have the chance to terrorize or end another woman's life.

BLONDE BUTCHER : The True Story of Ruth Judd

ERIN SPENCER

In 1931, Winnie Ruth Judd killed two of her best friends then cut one of them into pieces. She packed their remains inside two storage trunks and boarded a train for Los Angeles with the dead bodies as "luggage".

The media circus surrounding her crime was a parallel of the O.J. Simpson case in the mid-1990s. Reporters and readers alike were hungry for every sordid detail. Ruth, as she was known to her friends, would be tried and sentenced for execution until being declared mentally incompetent. She would later be remanded to the care of the Arizona State mental hospital where she would "escape" over seven times. During her last escape, she would journey to northern California where she would adopt an alias and avoid detect for over six years before her recapture.

CHAPTER ONE – EARLY LIFE

Winnie Judd was born Winnie Ruth McKinnell on January 29th, 1905. Born in Oxford, Indiana, her family soon moved from town to town as her father preached in different Methodist churches.

She suffered from tuberculosis as a child and was sent to an Arizona sanitarium for care. It was there that the seventeen year old would meet a thirty-seven year old physician named William Judd. They two would marry and Ruth would accompany him to Mexico where he was employed as a medic for American silver miners.

William, a World War I veteran, became a morphine addict in trying to cope with his injuries. The addiction soon seeped into his business life and he began having trouble holding down a job. The couple returned to the United States and began moving from city to city. The marriage was not a happy one as Ruth could not produce children and had repeated bouts with tuberculosis while William continued to struggle with his morphine addiction.

By 1930, the couple had a "needle separation", living apart but still remaining on talking terms. Winnie who had usually been called by her middle name, Ruth, had moved to Phoenix, Arizona where she hoped the drier climate would help with her tuberculosis. She had found work as a nanny to children with the Leigh Ford family, who were well-to-do. Upon her arrival in Phoenix, she met John "Happy Jack" Halloran, a successful businessman.

Halloran was married but was known for having open affairs.

John Halloran was nicknamed "Happy Jack" by the press when they got wind of his philandering ways. He was the co-founder of Halloran Bennett Lumber Company. A jowly man with a jovial personality, he used his wealth and status to procure young "party girls" despite the fact that he was married.

The two met while Ruth worked as a nanny for the Leigh Ford family. Jack lived next door with his wife and spotted the frail but pretty Ruth sitting on the Ford's front porch. He engaged the young woman in conversation and found out that her husband was away at a rehab center fighting another bout against his morphine addiction. Ruth confided to Jack that she was lonely and the opportunistic philanderer made his move.

They affair began on Christmas Eve of 1930 up until the night she murdered Anne and Sammy who were also involved with Jack.

Winnie would quit her job with the Ford family and obtain work as a medical secretary at the Grunow Medical Clinic in Phoenix.

It is here where she would befriend Agnes "Anne" Leroi, an x-ray technician and her roommate Hedvig "Sammy" Samuelson.

The two women had moved to Phoenix from Alaska as they wanted a better climate after Sammy had contracted tuberculosis.

The trio would have a tumultuous friendship that hinted of a love triangle between Annie, Ruth and Jack as well as a hints of homosexuality.

CHAPTER TWO – A TRIANGLE OF LUST

Ruth become close with Annie and Sammy, often having sleepovers at their bungalow. The two women soon become friends with Jack who, being the philanderer that he was, quickly indulged in relations with Annie.

This didn't sit well with Ruth who mistakenly believed that Jack loved her.

On October 16th, 1931, neighbors heard screaming coming from the bungalow. But the yelling stopped as quickly as it started and no one reported the fracas.

"I had introduced Jack to a girl they (Annie/Sammy) objected to," Winnie said in a jailhouse interview. "That is what the quarrel was over. He (Halloran) was a friend of my husband but he was trying to kiss my behind my husband's back. And I loved my husband very much."

Ruth had shot both women in a jealous fit with a .25 caliber handgun.

She then dismembered Sammy's body and put her head, torso, and lower legs into a shipping trunk while placing her thighs in a traveling suitcase. Annie's body was not dismembered, instead being stuffed into another shipping trunk.

The morning after, Ruth showed up late for work at the clinic while her co-workers wondered about the whereabouts of Annie. Later at the trial, some workers reported seeing Ruth as having a bandage on her left hand. Some remembered it being on her right. Others didn't remember it at all.

After her shift ended, Ruth called a moving van to retrieve a pair of large trunks and have them placed on a train for Los Angeles two days after the murders.

Ruth boarded the Golden State Limited passenger train at Phoenix's Union Station with both the trunk and suitcase which contained the bodies. She arrived in Los Angeles but her trunks immediately brought suspicion as porters saw the "stained fluid" coming from the trunks which was emitting a foul smell as well.

The porter, a man named Arthur Anderson, confronted Ruth.

"Ma'am," the porter said. "There's something leaking out of your trunk."

"Is there?"

"You know, a lot of folks try to transport contraband into Los Angeles," the train agent continued. "I've seen it all. Had one big game hunter use his wife to transport a dead deer. You wouldn't do something like that would you?"

"God, no."

"Do you have the keys for the trunk?"

"Its in my car."

"Let's open it please."

"My car is just outside," Ruth said, heading out of the depot. "Just wait right here. I'll get my keys, unlock the trunk and then I'll see what's leaking."

Ruth's younger brother Burton arrived in his vehicle to pick her up. Burton, a USC college student, had no idea that Ruth just committed murder.

"Drive," Ruth commanded.

"Where's all your stuff?" Burton asked.

"Just drive, Burton! Don't ask any questions, just go."

The car sped away as Anderson stepped out of the depot. He had the presence of mind to memorize the license plate of the vehicle and immediately reported the incident to the Los Angeles Police Department.

The police arrived, picked the locks on each of the trunks and were shocked to discovered the dead bodies inside.

"I was the chief investigator of the case," retired Phoenix detective Charles Arnold said. "From the police department in Phoenix at the time it happened. At the time it happened, the Phoenix police department knew nothing of Ruth Judd. Never heard of her. Until our police chief, that morning, received a call about nine o'clock, received a call from the captain of homicide from Los Angeles. The chief had said that they had discovered these trunks with nude bodies in them at the depot."

The police traced the car to Ruth's brother but the woman herself had disappeared. Ruth had gone home with Burton then hid in a department store among other places.

CHAPTER THREE – THE TRUNK MURDERS

The horrific crime would send shock waves throughout the country. The press would refer to Winnie as "Tiger Woman", "Blonde Butcher", and finally the case became known simply as the "Trunk Murders."

On Monday, October 19th, 1931, the Phoenix police force entered the home of Agnes and Sammy. Neighbors and reporters were also on the premises, disturbing the crime scene. The next day, the landlord of the bungalow placed an advertisement in two newspapers informing the public that he would be doing tours of the crime scene for ten cents per person.

Because of the ad, hundreds of people came through the bungalow out of morbid curiosity.

With their forensic evidence now contaminated, police nonetheless believed that both Annie and Sammy were shot while asleep in their beds. Both of their mattresses were missing from the bungalow but one was later found in a vacant lot a few miles away with no blood on it. The other mattress remained missing.

Police would also find a letter that Ruth had written to her husband but never mailed. The letter described a multitude of sexual goings-on at the Phoenix bungalow. Ruth would detail straight, bisexual and homosexual trysts that the trio would engage in.

With his wife now a wanted woman, Dr. William Judd put forth a public appeal for his Ruth to turn herself in.

Winnie caught word of her wanted status and would meet with police on October 23rd in a Los Angeles funeral home.

Detective Arnold led the interrogation of Ruthie as they spoke to her in the funeral home.

"Mrs, Judd, don't you think if a doctor amputated these bodies he would have known where to cut them and had to cut four and five places to find the joint?" Arnold asked.

Ruth shifted in her seat. "Well, it wasn't the doctor. I'll tell you who it was. It was Jack Halloran. Jack helped."

"How did you get the mattress out to the vacant lot that the women were laying on when you shot them?"

"I never shot no woman on a mattress!"

"Oh, yea, Ruthie, you shot women on the mattress. Because we found a mattress out on a vacant lot where you set it afire. And it hadn't burned up. And that was where the two women were laying side by each on this mattress. Because the blood spots were in two different spots on the mattress. And now, matter of fact, these women were sound asleep when you shot them weren't they?"

"No, no, they were fighting me."

"Ruthie, they wasn't fighting you. How could they be fighting you when you had them both in the bed there and you shot them straight down through the bed because the gunshots went through the mattress? How do you account for that Ruthie?"

Ruthie sat and stared at the ground. "Well, Jack Halloran helped me do it. And he said I should do that in order to get rid of the bodies."

"I said a while ago you told us that a doctor did that. Now Ruthie your story is all wet," Arnold shifted forward in his seat, narrowing his eyes. "Let me tell you the story. You went out there with this gun to kill these women because this one woman had rejected your love isn't that right? You found them sound asleep and you had the key to the door so you went quietly in there to where they were sleeping and you shot them right through the bed there. Because on this mattress that you drug out to the vacant lot and tried to burn there's two spots of blood not one, not a big spot, not a little spot but two spots in the mattress where the hole went through. Ain't that right, Ruthie?"

Tears began to well in Ruth's eyes. She gulped hard.

"Then you cut them up back there in the bath tub, you want to make this story good about fighting so I said you shot yourself through the hand, didn't you?"

"No, no, no, I never had any gun."

"Oh yes, Ruthie, you had a gun. A little automatic. Same gun you shot the women with. I found the bullet under bathtub that you shot yourself through the hand with."

Ruth broke down and began to cry. "I'm not telling you anything. I'm not saying anything. I'm not talking to you again, ever!"

Upon her arrest, Ruth became the O.J. Simpson of her day. The people of the 1930s were unused to the immorality depicted in Judd's crime-murder, infidelity, lesbianism, and drug use. They was conjecture that Agnes "Anne" and Hedvig "Sammy" Samuelson were "lesbian party girls" who seduced Ruth into their lifestyle of debauchery and perversion along with their mutual boyfriend, Jack Halloran.

CHAPTER FOUR – SELF DEFENSE OR PRE-MEDIATION?

Ruth would describe her murders of Annie and Sammy as incidents of self-defense. She described getting into an altercation with Sammy initially, describing how Sammy took out a gun and threatened to blow her brains out. Ruth said that she fought back and they both struggled with the gun.

"I went into the kitchen to set down some tapioca dessert," Winnie recalled. "We were all in our pajamas. I went to put this down on the sink and Sammy came at me with a gun. She came through the breakfast room door."

"We quarreled violently," Winnie said. "About what I was going to tell about them and what they were going to tell my husband about me and so forth. That I had gone out with Jack. So the fact that it took place in the breakfast room door. I'm naturally left handed. I do many things with my left hand. I grabbed the gun with this hand (her left) and the shot went through there (her palm.)And I grabbed a bread knife on the table and I stabbed her twice in the (left) shoulder. And the knife bent, it was a bread knife, so I grabbed her hand like this (pulling her wrist back) and we both had our hands on the gun and one shot went through one of her fingers. I don't know which one. And one went through her chest. And one bullet jammed and caught me here (her left ring finger), at the top of the gun. And Ann came from behind. She got the ironing board from behind the water heater and came up behind me and hit me which caused us both to fall in the doorway. And we fought back and forth, wrestling for the gun in the door way, both of us on the floor. And the blood was all underneath the linoleum that was the only way it got there it was from the fight. She was not shot in bed like they say! It was in the doorway and the kitchen. It wasn't in the bedroom at all."

Ruth then called Jack to help dispose of the dead bodies.

"Jack cut up Sammy's body," Ruth said initially. "I couldn't do it."

She would later recant on that claim and state that Jack Halloran had called up a "Dr. Brown" and had him come over to cut up the bodies. She said that Halloran had some "dirt" on the doctor which coerced the physician to come over to the home and become complicit in the murder.

"Jack came with me," Ruth said. "And he picked Sammy up and carried her in (to the bed). And he got Doctor Brown. They took me home because I was hysterical."

Ruth would also claim later that she had gone to Anne and Sammy's home for a game of bridge. A fourth woman was there but had left. She testified that there was an argument about Halloran's introduction to another woman and that Annie and Sammy attacked her.

Ruth stated that Halloran came to the bungalow and after seeing the bodies, began plotting a way to "fix things". He went to the garage and came back with a "great, heavy trunk".

"Don't say a word to anyone," he warned her.

Halloran would be blamed for being an accomplice in the crime but after further research the decision not to prosecute him seemed to be the right one, particularly with the half-baked imagination of Ruth.

Her stories would remain inconsistent during her interrogation with Detective Arnold as well.

"So we interviewed her for about an hour," Arnold recalled. "And she'd tell us one story and we'd head her off on that. And then she'd sit there for a few minutes and she'd say well, 'That's right, but I'm gonna tell you the truth now!' And she'd tell us another story. We asked her 'where's the knife that you used to cut these women up with?' 'I never cut no women up!' 'Oh yes, yes you must have because there were in your trunk. Where's the knife?' 'I never had any knife.' 'Well who cut the women up?' 'Well, the doctor cut 'em up.' 'A doctor helped you cut them up?' 'No, a doctor cut them up. He was there. He's my friend.'

It was discovered during the investigation that Jack Halloran and Ruth were having an affair. Halloran himself became under suspicion for the killings and was indicted by a grand jury on December 30th, 1932.

Ruth would become the primary witness through a preliminary hearing which lasted three days.

"I am going to be hanged for something Jack Halloran is responsible for," Winnie said. *"I was convicted of murder, but I shot in self-defense[1]. Jack Halloran removed every bit of evidence. He is responsible for me going through all this. He is guilty of anything I am guilty of."*

Even Dr. Judd, the husband of Ruth, believed that the man with whom is wife cheated with was not capable of the crime.

"I know Jack Halloran," Dr. Judd said. "And it is very difficult for me to believe that Jack had anything to do with that."

Halloran did not bother to take the stand during his hearing. His attorney informed the court that Ruth's stories were the rantings of a crazy woman. He argued further that since Winnie claimed that she

---

1.   *https://en.wikipedia.org/wiki/Self-defense*

killed the two women in self-defense there was no crime committed and Halloran was guilty of nothing.

The judge agreed, freeing Halloran in the belief that putting him to trial would be "an idle gesture."

"Jack Halloran had no more to do with the case than I did," Detective Arnold said. "She tried to involve Jack Halloran to get him to finance her defense. And when she fell down on it well, naturally she told a story that Jack helped her cut up the bodies and so on. But she already told that a doctor that helped her but she never would give us the doctor's name."

The controversy surrounding the case did irreparable damage to Halloran's reputation. He would lose valuable business contacts and his social standing in the community. Six years later, he would die at suddenly at the age of fifty-two.

CHAPTER FIVE – A LETTER OF CONFESSION

In 1931, Ruth would write out her "true confession" letter below and deliver it to her attorney. This letter detailed both the events of the night of the murder and her thought processes. Her attorney, Howard Richardson, did not use the letter. He instead had it "buried" as he tried to get her off on an insanity plea.

"I am writing the absolute truth of this case, in full confidence, that you will use it as you see fit in your best judgment. Mr. Richardson, I have full confidence in you and trust you.

This is my first and only confession of the case of the homicide of Anne LeRoi and Hedvig Samuelson. Anne was used to the world, I truly was not. Jack was the only man I had gone with since my marriage. I was ashamed of things I had done. I could not openly compete with her, I was married and ashamed to. Day after day she lorded it over me, always smiling and fresh and sweet, well knowing she was hurting me with her taunts. Many evenings Anne would kiss Jack and caress him in our presence, then after he was gone gloat over not caring a thing for him but merely working him for money. It was not what Jack did but the continual taunts made by Anne which drove me beside myself... I could not stand taunts. I just went crazy. Those taunts kept me awake, I could not sleep. I cried. I even prayed. I wrote my parents to please come to me. I was losing my mind. Wild ideas kept me awake. I took sleeping sedatives, Luminal. I wrote Doctor my nerves were breaking. I couldn't eat. I couldn't sleep. I loved Anne still, but those taunts. I would take more medicine to quiet my nerves, cried to please get things off my mind, to sleep. Friday night I expected Jack. He did not come. I went to bed. Again I could not sleep. I got up, went over to Anne's house. My brain whirling. I was so excited I was panting for breath. Never did I have the slightest dream of hurting Sammy. She simply never entered my mind. Except to get Anne, stop those taunts so I could sleep. Nothing more did I think of. I took the gun and a knife. How I would do it I was not sure. But I had no intention of harming Sammy. Jack was as intimate with Sammy as Anne, but it was Anne's cruel taunts that haunted me.... I hid in the house next door. Anne and Sammy returned to the bedroom . . . After they retired, I went to the back door, laid the knife and my shoes outside the door, then crept in the unlocked front door . . . I sat down on the couch in the same dark room and soon fell to sleep clutching the gun. I awakened, Sammy had gone to the bathroom, that insane desire, that power lead me on, I started for Anne. My stomach was turning inside out really twitching, jumping out of me, outside not a tremor, but my stomach jumping like convulsions. I retreated, curled up and went to sleep again. I went back to sleep again. Oh again and again all night I don't know how many times. Sammy kept going to the bathroom, I started for that bedroom and retreated each time so exhausted I immediately went to sleep.

Morning! I heard the milk man. Sammy went to the bathroom again. I started to call her, tell her I was there. I really did. Then I began shaking inside and remembered what I had come to do so this time I crept past the bathroom door, shot Anne. It was a low shot. Sammy called, What fell, Anne? I was hurrying past the door Sammy came out demanded to know what was the matter. I was limp she completely took the gun from my hands. I was non-resistant. I said, Sammy, I am crazy. I have lost my mind give me that gun and I will blow my brains out right here in this door. She held the gun and said, you get out of here right this minute.

... I then picked up the knife and went back after her with the knife. As I grabbed for the gun, I stabbed her in the shoulder, the fight with Sammy in that breakfast room door; her own finger on the trigger when the shot went through her chest; our fight is all about as I have always related she shot me through the hand as I grabbed for the gun; the gun jammed; we fell to the floor, struggled and I finally got the gun and shot her and in my wild state I really do not remember where in the head. I pulled Sammy into the bathroom. I cleaned up the floor I pulled in the trunk from the garage. It was now about 6:30 or 7 a.m. . . . I tugged and pulled and finally got Anne from the bed into the trunk. Now it doesn't sound possible but this all took about two hours. I left for the office . . . I had pulled the trunk with Anne's body into the living room. But the trunk was unlocked. Sammy was on the bathroom floor all day Saturday . . . This all happened in the morning. I stayed in my office . . . until 4 p.m. I then took the bag home with me with the gun, knife, pajamas and dress. I fed my cat and went back to the 2929 N. 2nd Street house at around 6 p.m. I really had nothing definite in my mind. No plans made. In fact except for an irresistible impulse to get Anne I had no other plans. I entered the house through the bathroom window getting a chair from next door to climb in. I pulled the trunk back into the hall tried to lift Sammy into it, but that was utterly impossible, I couldn't possibly lift her, she was too heavy her body was stiff. I then got two cheap knives from the kitchen and severed her body into portions I could lift. I was hours doing this and then inch by inch pulling the trunk back into the living room."

CHAPTER SIX – THE TRIAL

Three months after the bodies had been discovered, Judd's trial began. Ruth would not be tried for the murder of Sammy, only the murder of Agnes.

Richardson would be steadfast in his defense that Ruth was innocent by reason of insanity. He didn't allow her to take the stand. He kept the existence of Ruth's confessional letter to himself.

The case went to trial with the prosecutors taking aim at Ruth's self-defense alibi. They pointed out the fact that Ruth did not have a bullet wound in her hand when she showed up for work the day after and that her wound was, in fact, self-inflicted to confuse authorities. They further argued that Ruth killed the two women out of a jealous rage as she did not want her husband to find out about her affair with Jack Halloran.

The jurors agreed with the prosecution and found Ruth guilty of two counts of first-degree murder.

She was sentenced to death by hanging.

Ruth then behaved oddly in jail, screaming, yelling and making bizarre gestures. Because of her high-profile case, the Arizona governor gave her a special sanity hearing that took place only three days before her scheduled death-by-hanging.

This hearing became a spectacle for the media. Ruth put on a show, laughing inappropriately, clapping her hands, screaming obscenities at the jury and pulling out clumps of her hair. She then tried to take off her clothes and had to be restrained.

"She's been crazy all her life," Ruth's mother would testify during the hearing. "More or less."

"She comes from a long, lineage of crazy folk," Winnie's father, the Methodist preacher revealed. "Our family has been cursed with madness for over 125 years. It goes all the way back to Scotland."

The testimony worked and Ruth's death sentence was commuted to a life prison term. She was then sent to an Arizona state hospital for the criminally insane.

CHAPTER SEVEN – FUGITIVE ON THE RUN

Ruth would show a dramatic improvement in her mental stability during her stay at the hospital. She no longer displayed the same screaming fits or displays of anger. She fit in with the prison population and embrace the routine, all the while calculating ways to escape.

She left behind a "dummy" in her bed, made up of items around the sanitarium. Fooling the guards, she slipped out of the mental hospital only to be recaptured days later.

The prison guards had her on close watch upon her return but Ruth was determined.

She would escape a total of seven times. On one occasion, Ruth walked all the way from Phoenix to Yuma, Arizona, making her way along the Southern Pacific railroad tracks. These escapes would become a national joke because on slow news days reporters would remark, "maybe Winnie Ruth Judd will escape again."

These escapes would become a running gag among the more sensationalist newspapers. One magazine opened an article on Judd with the words : "When you read this story, the country's cleverest maniac may be at large again, perhaps walking down your street, or sitting next to you."

Ruth would return to her sanitarium after another escape in 1952. Inexplicably, she would be called to testify before a grand jury that was investigating state hospital conditions.

Ever the opportunist, Ruth would plot out another escape during her transport to the hearing. She was searched beforehand, however, and prison guards found a key hidden in her hair and a razor blade concealed beneath her tongue.

A year later, Ruth would have another sanity hearing. During this time she would spent a great deal of time trying to obtain her letter of confession back from her attorney Howard Robinson's widow to get this letter back. She had enough wherewithal to realize that if the letter would be made public it would be incriminating evidence against her insanity defense.

Richardson's widow did not comply but the letter would not be revealed until after Ruth's death.

CHAPTER EIGHT – THE GREAT ESCAPE

Ruth would stage her most successful escape on October 8th, 1963. She coerced a friend to give her the key to the front door of the hospital and made her way out undetected in the middle of the night.

"About these seven escapes," Arnold said. "The woman, in my opinion, its just my opinion, but I've been around. This woman never escaped out there. She was turned loose every time she went away from that asylum. They wanted to get rid of her! And she wasn't getting seen very fast according to their opinion. And every time she went out of there she'd go out and try to get money from some of her old friends to leave town on and she couldn't get the money. Then somebody would see her and turn her in and then of course the hospital would have to go back and get her. And put her back in the hospital. And that was carried on there for a number of years as I say as everybody knows she's supposedly escaped from there seven times. Before she got enough money to leave town on (laughs)."

Ruth somehow made her way from the Arizona sanitariums to the San Francisco Bay Area where she took on the name of "Marian Lane."

She lived with the wealthy Nichols family, finding work as their live-in maid.

"One of the reasons I came here (to San Francisco) was to be near him (her husband)," Winnie said. "He's buried here in the Golden Gate National Military Cemetery. And when I go down there frequently, I put violets on his grave. I thought he was a wonderful person. He was ill and he was worth saving. And I worked very hard. Ms. Nickles knew I loved violets so she had a whole lot planted so I could pick them anytime and take them to his grave. Because I was buying violets and she said I'll plant the violets, she was that kind and good to me."

Her identity was eventually discovered and she was recaptured after six years of freedom. Ruth would hire attorney Melvin Belli to represent her and he fought her extradition to Arizona. Governor

Ronald Reagan, however, personally intervened, sending Ruth back to Arizona.

Ruth would be tried again and judged sane, thus ending her stays at sanitariums. She was sent to jail but only incarcerated for an additional two years.

Ruth would be paroled on December 22nd, 1971. Upon her release she moved to Stockton, California where she lived out the rest of her life without incident. In 1983, the state of Arizona gave her an "absolute discharge" which meant that she was no longer a parolee of the state.

Winnie Ruth Judd would die on October 23rd, 1998 at the age of ninety-three.

THE SCUMBAG

Alexis Malone

Gary Charles Evans was born to Roy Evans and Flora Mae Lee in Troy, New York on October 7th, 1954. He had an older half sister named Robbie who was the product of a previous relationship for his mother. There was also a family friend named Jo Realm who was considered his "older sister."

Gary wore thick glasses in school and was teased. His father also subjected him to regular beatings whenever Gary disobeyed him. He would beat the boy unmercifully with a leather strap, making welts form across his back.

Roy was an Army corps pilot until being discharged. He was aimless after his military service ended, working as a bartender but then becoming permanently disabled after flying head first through a car windshield in an accident. He would then take out his life's frustrations on his family, particularly Gary.

Roy Evans would often make his son stay at the dinner table until he finished his food. There were occasions when he would tie him to the dining room chair and force feed liver to Gary.

Gary would also allege that his father would sexually assault him, "doing vile things" which he "wouldn't wish on anyone."

His parents would have violent arguments and forced Gary to stay in his room, confining him like the future prisoner he would become. He would not be allowed to watch television, draw or do any other pursuits which may have interested him.

His "big sister", Jo Realm, would give him food, passing dinner plates from her room to his because their apartments were so close.

His mother, Flora, worked primarily in retail and in a factory. The factory she worked for closed down, however, so Flora turned to housekeeping to make ends meet.

Flora suffered from mental illness and attempted suicide several times. She would often make these suicide threats in front of both Gary and his sister, traumatizing them. On one occasion, she waved a gun around, threatening to kill herself. When her husband tried to intervene she accidentally shot him in the shoulder.

Flora would have scars on her wrists from slitting them so many times. She would bring men home and make Gary stand watch outside the door while they had sex.

His mother would continue her suicidal ways, one time she threatened to jump off the roof of their apartment building but Robbie tearfully talked her out of it. Sometimes Flora would wander to the railroad tracks and stand in the crossroad, waiting for the train to come run her over.

Robbie would again talk her out of it, convincing her how much she and Gary loved her.

"The whole nature versus nurture argument comes to bear in looking at Gary's background," forensic psychologist Wendy Lipscomb said. "He was abused by his father physically and perhaps sexually. This coupled with the mental abuse by his mother made the wiring in his brain abnormal, without question. He had no one to turn to for guidance really other than his sisters Robbie and big sister Jo. He would remain wired that way for the rest of his life, having more of an ability to relate to women more so than men. His victims would all be men."

Gary's life of crime would start at the age of eight. He had stolen a ring worth over $1,000 in addition to comic books and toys. His mother was a thief herself, shoplifting items at will.

The constant bickering between his parents would end when Gary was fourteen years old as they would finally divorce.

Flora would remarry and divorce four more times over the next three years. She had Gary would move to Potterville, New York but her new husband would prove to be an abusive alcoholic. Later, she would marry a man named "Jim" who was another alcoholic. Going through another divorce, Flora declared herself to be a lesbian and got a girlfriend.

Gary would be forced to live with his older sister (Robbie) and her husband.

His brother-in-law was prone to violence, abusing both Gary and his sister. This would force Gary out onto the streets where he would fend for himself, ping-ponging between the streets and his mother's home.

Gary began to support himself by whatever means he could, mostly by stealing from drug dealers to obtain money. At the age of sixteen, he broke into a home and serve three months for the burglary.

By the mid-1970s, Gary would spend a lot of time being homeless. He would break into cars, trucks, and abandoned buildings. Eventually, he would live with two childhood friends. One was a man named Michael Falco who reportedly tortured and sexually abused animals. The other was fellow thief, Timothy Rysedorph. Gary would live in a shed behind their apartment before he moved in.

"They played baseball or stick ball or something when they were little kids," Dana Rysedorph, the wife of Tim said. "They rode their bikes together and did the things that little kids do. And they may have shared an apartment when (Rysedorph) was about 19."

"But since I started dating Tim, I never saw the man (Gary Evans)," Dana said. "The first time I saw the man was when the police showed me a mug shot. I'd like to know when Tim had time to fit this in. All he ever did was work and spend time with us. But because he knew (Evans, he's supposed to be side-by-side with him?"

Having these two partners in crime, Gary would step up his thievery, becoming adept at appraising antiques and jewelry. He would run a con on local antique dealers, pretending to be an expert. He would study their storefronts for openings in which he could later break in.

Both Falco and Rysedorph would assist him in these antique store burglaries. The trio would bypass store alarms by tunneling outside the walls in order to enter the store undetected.

Evans would be convicted for fifteen antique-store robberies over the course of his life.

"Gary was the ringleader of the group of friends from around his block," Lipscomb said. "He held no emotions for them, however. He viewed them as a means to an end, people that he could use and later discard if they proved to be a liability. For the most part, he was a loner. He could sleep out in the woods and go for long periods of time without the need for any contact. He didn't so much have friendships with men as much as he had partners in crime."

Gary would have many girlfriends, mainly Deirdre Fuller. The two would date from 1977 until 1990 but the relationship would be a tumultuous one. He was okay with her dating other men, as long as they were Caucasian. When Deirdre began dating a black man, Gary became enraged.

He wanted everything he had ever given her back.

"I would like to kill a woman and a nigger," he would later state to friends.

On January 13th, 1977, Gary would be caught burglarizing a home in Lake Place, New York. He would be sentenced to four years in prison, being held at the Clinton Correctional Facility in Dannemora, New York.

Six months later, his father would die of throat cancer while Gary was held in jail.

He would serve two years of the four year sentence until his release. When he got out, he went back into the same pattern of petty theft with Tim Rysedorph and Michael Falco.

They would use their apartment as a fencing headquarters for all of their stolen goods before renting out a storage unit.

The trio would evade capture for almost a year until Gary was stopped by police and caught with a few hundred dollars in stolen goods.

Gary, still on parole, was immediately sent back to prison, this time to the old Rensselaer County Jail in downtown Troy, New York.

On this occasion, however, he would befriend some Hells Angels inside who engineered an escape. Gary would be captured five hours after fleeing the prison and be punished with solitary confinement.

Gary would remain in prison and be denied parole this time around.

The New York State Department of Corrections then transferred him to Attica State Prison which housed the most violent criminals. Gary was spared being placed in the general population but it is here that Jim Horton, the chief investigator of his crimes, believed that Gary turned violent.

He would work as an informant for Jim Horton, telling them of impending petty crimes that he knew were about to take place, setting up a large drug bust with a man named Archie Bennett.

"Gary was a good talker when he wanted to be," Lipscomb said. "He knew he could charm and he couldn't. By running cons in the antique business, he quickly learned the art of negotiation. He was able to parlay this skill in getting a 'job' of sorts as an informant."

Gary would be released from prison on December 29th, 1982 but once again return to his old pals, particularly Michael Falco.

Two months later, however, Gary's mother would die in a freak accident. She fell on some ice while entering her car and hit her head on the bumper.

Gary grieved but soon returned to his life of crime with Falco and Rysedorph. He would break into a home on Easter, 1983 and once again be arrested.

Back in prison, he remained there for a year before being set free on a "conditional release program." This mandated that he had to be on his best behavior for the remaining nine months of his sentence.

Gary would scoff at the court order. He went back to burglarizing homes as soon as he was released. Teaming up with Falco, the two thieves would not get caught over the next nine months.

On February 16th, 1985, the duo would go to East Greenbush, New York in Falco's brown Plymouth. They had two large duffel bags, a police scanner, a rope ladder and other burglary tools.

Parking behind an antique shop, they propped up a portable toilet and made their way to the top of the roof.

Gary and Falco then dropped down from a hatch on the roof. In just minutes, they would fill the duffel bags with whatever they could; gold, jewelry, valuables all tallying up to $15,000.

They climbed back out of the store and whooped and hollered at the size of their stolen booty.

A cop, however, pulled up behind them as they were about to leave.

He asked what they were doing behind the building and the two men casually explained that they had to "take a piss."

The cop took their identification down and let the two thieves go, Gary's charm enabling them to get away.

"At this point of his life, Gary was a career criminal," Lipscomb said. "He was intelligent, with the ability to meticulously plan a robbery. He could walk into a store and see the ways in and out, ways in which the ordinary person would never dream. But for all this intelligence he could not see the trajectory that his life was on. He was only intelligent in certain things. He did not have a clue when it came to living a sustainable life. He was one a road destined to prison and true to like minded criminals he did nothing to get off that path. He embraced it instead."

On April 21st, 1985, Gary went to Troy, New York to sell dope to two marijuana dealers. The dealers gave him the money ($12,000) and when they went to his trunk to retrieve the marijuana, Gary sprinted away. The two men gave chase and Gary circled back around, getting into their vehicle and speeding away.

The dope dealers then called the police, telling them that Gary had robbed them of both the money and the car by gunpoint.

Making his way into Cohoes, New York, Gary would run a red light.

A cop immediately pulled him over but Gary thought the officer was stopping him for the robbery. Gary then threw his gun and fake identification out of the vehicle before sprinting out of the car. The cops eventually found him and sent him to the Albany County Jail.

On July 1985, he was sentenced to another two to four years before being moved to the Renssaler County Jail.

Upon his release, Gary would commit his first murder in shooting his burglary partner, Michael Falco. Rysedorph had told Gary that Falco had stolen some jewelry from him. Rysedorph said that Falco had given the jewelry to a female friend. This enraged Gary and he decided to kill his childhood friend.

Gary would use a .22 caliber pistol with a homemade silencer (he would make the silencer himself with parts of a screen door and duct tape)

He enlisted the aid of Rysedorph to put Falco's body in the trunk of his own car, wrapping the corpse up in a sleeping bag.

The two then drove to Lake Worth, Florida to visit Gary's sister Robbie.

They would bury the body near her house and would stay in Florida. It would later be revealed that Rysedorph had lied and the truth was that he had stolen the jewelry.

"Gary had now made the progression from small-time thief to drug dealer and murderer," Lipscomb said. "This does fit the psychological profile given his background. He endured parental abuse and would torture animals (he once tied up the tail of a cat and set it on fire.)

Bouncing in and out of jail had no doubt lowered his inhibitions. Whatever remorse or hesitation he felt was now out the window. He would commit whatever crime he felt would be necessary and his mindset would be the same. 'Don't get caught, don't get caught.' If anyone around him was careless or looked like they would prospectively betray him, they would be killed. Falco was the first of many."

Gary would then return to prison after being caught for another burglary. His sister Robbie would write Gary in prison. She wouldn't visit and hardly ever wrote so Gary was scratching his head upon receiving her letter. Robbie would write that someone was calling her, disguising their voice as Gary's. This person would say that he was into bestiality and bragged about having sex with farm animals.

It was yet another episode in an increasing series of bizarre occurrences in Gary's life. While in prison, he began fantasizing about an ex-girlfriend, Stacy, someone he had not seen in over fifteen years. Gary wanted to find her and then kill anyone who got in his way who tried to stop him. Gary would never admit to being homosexual but it was reported that he had relationships with transsexuals in prison. Later, he would have a friend come over and discover his collection of homosexual magazines, dildos and other gay sex toys.

In December of 1986, Gary would be moved to the Clinton Correctional Facility. He was placed under protective custody as he convinced authorities that the Hells Angels were out to kill him.

Gary would complain that he was being held until March of 1988 when his release date should have been in December of 1987. He then wrote a letter to Torri Ellis (Falco's common-law wife) and inquired if she heard anything about Falco, knowing full well that he killed the man.

While in prison, Gary would befriend David "The Son Of Sam" Berkowitz who was a serial killer of young girls. David would call Gary "The Great Tricep King" in reference to his muscular arms. The serial killer would anger Gary, however, when he gave him a muscle magazine which featured a black bodybuilder. David would later apologize to Gary as he didn't realize how racist his fellow mate was.

The two would lift weights together but during one session Gary would call his new friend "David Berserk-o-witz" which would end up in a shouting match between the two.

His troubles in jail didn't end with the Son of Sam. Beefed up with the weight training, Gary entered a child molester's cell and "body slammed him all over."

He was then sent to solitary confinement for two weeks before being once again released in March of 1988.

"During this last foray in prison, Gary would come out even more sociopathic than before," Lipscomb said. "He now had a new physique, building up his arms and back. He would use this to intimidate drug dealers in the area and his future partners in crime. It was a classic case of 'show me your friends and I'll show you your future.' He had spent the majority of his adult life amongst criminals in jail. Now, armed with a new physique, he would be ready to take his game to another level."

Gary would befriend a new partner in crime, Damien Cuomo, and the duo would pride themselves on being intelligent thieves. The pair would be smarter and more prolific than before, even going so far as wearing shoes that were three and four sizes too big to throw off the investigators.

As part of his parole, however, Gary had to get a job. He always thought jobs were for suckers and that they were "too hard."

Investigator Horton seemed to take pity on him, however, and set the lifetime thief up for different jobs. Gary would work at a cemetery digging holes but couldn't make it past the first five days. Ironically, while he was in prison, he was forced to work. Gary was an amateur artist and the prison authorities made him make greeting cards. This earned him $7 a week which he used to buy junk food with Twinkies being his favorite.

After the cemetery job fell through, Gary got a job at a garden nursery where he would do all of the heavy lifting. He worked sporadically, more comfortable with commiting burglaries on the side.

Gary would stay out of trouble for almost a year until March of 1989. He and Cuomo were on their way to a job when a cop pulled them over. The officer searched their trunk and found ski masks, stun guns, a police scanner, walkie-talkies, crowbars, screwdrivers, duct tape, ropes, handcuffs, gloves, hats, maps, and a book on police radio frequencies.

The cop did not discover that the duo had hidden stolen goods in the door panels and under a carpet in the trunk.

He did have enough to book the lifelong criminals, however.

"Gary was a hopeless case at this point," Lipscomb said. "He was advancing in age and could never adjust to a normal nine-to-five. He had disdain for an honest days work and preferred the quick hit of a burglary. At this point, he is also a travesty of the criminal justice system. He had been in and out of jail over twenty-three times, they still can't pin the Falco murder on him, yet they keep letting him out of jail."

After a brief jail term, Gary would be released and immediately pick up where he left off with Cuomo.

On September 8th of 1989, they would kill Douglas Berry, a store owner asleep in his shop after hours.

Gary and Cuomo did not realize that Berry was still in the store when they had broken in. Berry was asleep but the breaking glass awoke him. He discovered the two men in his store but Gary would shoot him once in the head with his .22 caliber gun.

The shot would be fatal.

The duo ran out of the store, leaving Berry's body in full view.

Gary would monitor the news with anxiety until police arrested another man for the murder. This innocent man was soon released, however, and the police remained in the dark in who shot Douglas Berry.

Three months later, Gary would kill his partner, Damien Cuomo. He believed that he should have gotten more money for their robbery as he only got $15,000. He shot him three times in the back of the head after handcuffing Cuomo's hands behind his back. He wrapped up Cuomo's body with a shower curtain, blanket and tied it all together with a rope.

Gary had dug a hole at his place weeks before and hid Cuomo's body inside, covering it with a makeshift door and dirt.

He then went on the run to Florida with his girlfriend, bringing her along so it looked as if he was not hiding something.

In the summer of 1990, he still had Stacy (his teenage girlfriend/ fantasy) on his mind. It had been over fifteen years since he had seen her and he daydreamed about taking her away from her husband

Gary followed up on his warped fantasy. He showed up at her workplace but Stacy made it clear that she did not want anything to do with him. He then went back to New York and in October of 1981, he would kill another jewelry shop owner named Gregory Jouben.

This killing would be pre-planned.

Gary entered the store and pretended that he was looking to by some jewelry. He waited until Jouben looked down to retrieve a piece when Gary shot him three times in the back of the head with his .22 caliber pistol.

Gary had placed a pillow case around his gun to catch the shells. He would then steal over $60,000 worth of valuables from Jouben.

In a panic, the now confirmed serial killer would flee to Colorado but then return. He placed the gun that he killed Jouben with into a metal box and buried it in the back of Albany Rural Cemetery.

Always the opportunist, Gary would steal a marble bench from the cemetery (it weighed one thousand pounds) and bring it back to New York, successfully selling it days later. He would also steal a 300-pound brass eagle which stood atop an obelisk marking Col. Ernest Ellsworth's grave.

"With the killing of Cuomo," Lipscomb said. "Gary no longer had a regular partner. So he had to strong arm some of his burglaries as was the case with the Jouben murder. He wouldn't be able to break in by himself so instead he takes a more direct approach. This new bold attitude bespeaks of his growing arrogance. Even if he goes to jail he will come right back out. He's a man that will steal anything that isn't nailed down. Even if it is nailed down, he'll try and take out the nails."

In March of 1993, Gary would break into the bathroom window of the antique shop of Kathy Alexander. He would steal diamonds, gold, a rare handbag valuing up to $20,000.

For whatever reason, Gary had a fetish for hanging out in cemeteries. He would try to steal another marble bench from a cemetery but this time graveyard security spotted him. Once again, he would be throw in jail but only for a month.

Seeking new opportunities, he would break into the Norman Williams Public Library in Woodstock, Vermont and steal the Birds of America book by James Audubon. This was bad news for Gary as not only was the book priceless but a federal judge was on the Board of Trustees for the library. He would give himself up for stealing the book and be sentenced to 27 months in jail. Gary would serve only thirteen months and upon his release, he would kill his former partner Timothy Rysedorph.

Rysedorph was helping Gary clean out their storage facility where they kept their stolen goods. Gary then turned the gun on Rysedorph, killing him.

Rysedorph would reported missing by his wife, Dana.

He had called her earlier from a Dunkin Donuts restaurant and said he would be home within the hour. His car would be found the next day.

Rysedorph would leave a note on the table for his family which said "Have a good day. See you later. I love you."

Dana and his then nine year old son Timmy would hope for the best to no avail.

Gary had cut up Rysedorph's body with a chainsaw, sectioning the limbs off in five pieces. He bagged each body part then placed them into cardboard boxes. He then drove to a hill in Brunswick, New York where he buried the boxes in a shallow grave. He tossed the gun and chain saw into the Hudson river.

Gary would cover his tracks, deciding to call Lisa (Cuomo's girlfriend) and inquire about Tim Rysedorph.

"Lisa? Lisa Morris?"

"Yeah?"

"This is Lou," he said in an angry voice. "Where's Tim (Rysedorph)?"

"Who's this?"

"This Lou."

"I don't know. Who are you?"

"I'm a friend of his from work. I'm returning his call."

"I haven't heard from him."

"Hmmm," Gary said. "He might be in some trouble, girl. He might be in some trouble."

Still on probation, Gary disappeared for seven months. He would call Lisa again, telling her that what happened to Mike (Falco) probably happened to Tim (Rysedorph) but that Cuomo was probably living it up in the Carolinas. He would befriend the woman, giving her all kinds of stories of why Cuomo was not coming back. He needed a place to stay and she allowed him to live there.

Police would finally trace the killing of Rysedorph back to him. He would be captured in Jonesbury, Vermont.

Gary would confess to the five killings and then be transferred to Albany County jail where he would remain in protective lock down.

He would then lead detectives to where he buried the bodies of Tim Rysedorph and Damien Cuomo.

Investigator Jim Horton then made Gary call Lisa Morris again and tell her that he had killed Cuomo after having her believe for so long that he was still alive.

The woman was flabbergasted. She could not believe that Gary had lied to her and for so long.

Gary was transferred to the Rensselaer County Jail in downtown Troy but nixed the idea when they realized that that part of the jail was under reconstruction. He was considered a serious flight risk and admitted to both investigator Horton and Jo Rehm that he will try to escape.

The district attorney decided to try him as a capital offender and have him executed by lethal injection.

Gary would have his hearing at the Albany Jail in Colonie, New York. During his transport, he kicked out the window of the police van while the vehicle was traveling across the Troy-Menands bridge over the Hudson river.

"They were traveling about 60 miles an hour when he apparently threw both his feet through the window and shattered it," Troy Fire Chief Robert Essigan said. "Somehow he jumped out the window, over the guardrail and into the water."

Evans had his hands shackled behind him and his feet chained together as he was riding in the rear of the caged U.S. Marshals van.

The trip was only supposed to last twenty minutes. A second vehicle with two additional deputy U.S. Marshalls followed as Evans made his way back to the Rensselaer County Jail.

He then dove onto the roadway through the side window. The vehicles screeched to a halt.

Deputies then chased Evans who had "hobbled" over to the side of the road before jumping off the bridge.

Witnesses would call the police as they initially thought Evans was a construction worker with his orange coveralls.

Gary had taken off his handcuffs and flipped off the US Marshalls as he fell to his death.

"There was really nothing they could do," Essigan said. "This guy was quite an escape artist. He was good, and I guess this was his spectacular ending."

He left behind a suicide letter expressing regret that he would not be able to spend time with Doris Sheehan, the woman he loved.

His final words were sent to lawyer Randolph Treece, whom he addressed in a letter. "No lessons here are learned, onto a better place now," Evans wrote. "My friends are happy and I'm already there with Canis Minor (a star of the constellation Orion) and a Beautiful Blue Moon with a smile, stars surround me and peace and love are mine. They can't be taken or touched."

"I win," were the last words he wrote, underlining "win."

His body would be recovered and during the autopsy the medical examiner would find a razor blade and a paper clip taped to his ankle under his sock.

Gary also had a handcuff key stuffed up his left nasal passage with another razor blade shoved very deep inside his nose.

Relatives of his victims felt no remorse when they learned of Gary's suicide.

"It couldn't have happened to a nicer guy," Mary Deeb said, the sister of Michael Falco. "I'll probably go to hell for that but I can't help it. That's the way I felt. It's terrible to feel so relieved that someone jumped to his death but I cant help it."

"I'm going to tell you, when I saw him on TV and he had this very smug, arrogant, non-remorseful look on his face. I knew he's no good," Sal Falco said, the older brother of Michael. "I think there's a higher power that says it's time for you to stand in my court and there's a tougher jury up there."

"Forgive? Forgive him for killing my brother? No way. There's no reason to kill my brother. He didn't do anything wrong. He didn't deserve that kind of a sentence."

"He killed Michael when he was 26," Elaine DiMauro said, Falco's former girlfriend and mother of his two children. "He had a family and two children to look forward to. I was hoping he would go to jail. Justice still hasn't been served."

"I think the gates of hell are opening wide open for this man. The fires are burning pretty crisp. I hope to God they suffocate him."

SMELLY BOB

OSCAR VALDEZ

Robert Black (Smelly Bob)

Robert Black, also known as "Smelly Bob" was a Scottish pedophile and serial killer who preyed on young girls in the United Kingdom. Between 1981 and 1986, Black was convicted of the kidnap, sexual assault, and murder of four girls—plus the kidnapping and rape of another young girl and the attempted kidnapping of yet another—between the ages of five and 11 and was sentenced to life in prison with a minimum of 35 years. Black is also suspected of being responsible for the murders of 12 other girls between 1969 and 1987 in England, Ireland, and continental Europe. Black died of natural causes on 12 January 2016 while incarcerated at HMP Maghaberry, just weeks before he was to be charged with the murder of another of his victims.

Early Life

Robert Black was born on 21 April 1947 in Grangemouth, Stirlingshire, Scotland, the illegitimate son of Jessie Hunter Black who was 24 at the time and an unknown father whose name was never put on Black's birth certificate. Jessie earned a pittance as a factory worker and was in no position to care for a child, let alone an illegitimate one which carried with it a large social stigma. So, when he was six months old Black's mother had him fostered. He was subsequently raised by experienced, middle-aged couple Jack and Isabel Tulip who lived in Kinlochleven. Black initially adopted their surname and lived with them until 1958 when his foster mother died; his foster father having already passed away when Black was five. When Margaret died, Black was only 11 years of age.

In the meantime Black's mother married Francis Hall, had four more children who never even knew that they had a half-brother, and moved to Australia. She died in 1982 without ever having any contact with the son she gave away.

Locals remember how young Black was usually heavily-bruised as a child; however, Black himself does not remember how he sustained most of the injuries. He did recall how Margaret used to lock him in the house as punishment for poor behavior or would spank his bare bottom with a belt. During the night, Black feared that there was a monster under his bed and he suffered from a recurring nightmare that featured a "big hairy monster" in a cellar full of water. When he awakened, he found that he had typically wet the bed, for which he was invariably beaten.

In school he was referred to as "Smelly Robbie Tulip" and is remembered to this day as "aggressive and slightly wayward" as well as being a loner with a tendency to bully. Black preferred the company of younger children who he could easily dominate. Instead of joining a "gang" of classmates his age, he started his own and all of the members were several years younger than he. Compounding the problem was that Black demonstrated "sudden, mindless violence perpetrated against those physically less able than himself."

The local bobbie, Sandy Williams, remembers Black as a "wild wee laddie" who "didn't give a damn" or have respect for authority and that he had a "dangerous spirit" and "needed a smack round the ear to keep him in line." However, the entire time Black lived with the Tulips he was never in serious trouble; just childish fights, bullying younger children, swearing, and other normal trouble at school—nothing that merited more than a rebuke from Williams.

When Margaret died when Black was 11 years of age, it was one of the worst possible things imaginable because now he was, again, deprived of a mother. Black was subsequently placed with another foster family in Kinlochleven. He only lived with them a short time because not long after his placement he dragged a young girl into a public bathroom and sexually fondled her. His new foster mother reported the offense to social workers and insisted that Black be placed elsewhere. Black was then sent to the Redding Children's home, a mixed-gender children's home near Falkirk, close to where he was born.

From a young age Black exhibited significant antisocial tendencies, particularly a disturbing awareness of and fascination with sex and women's vaginas. At the age of five he and a girl compared their genitalia. At the age of seven at a school dance he preferred lying on the floor and staring up girls' dresses instead of actually dancing. At the age of eight he took off a neighbor's baby's diaper while he was babysitting to look at her vagina. Despite being heterosexual, Black stated that he would have preferred to have been born female; not that he had any feminine tendencies but he simply hated his penis and would have preferred having a vagina instead. In a prison interview after he was convicted for his heinous crimes, Black confessed to enjoy pushing things up his anus and following his arrest in 1990, police found photographs Black had taken of himself with various unusual objects inserted in his anus. He also confessed to a preoccupation with feces. If one attributed classical Freudian personality psychology, that Black had a tendency to withhold emotion, was oftentimes smelly and messy, and was preoccupied with his anus, then he would be the epitome of an anal personality type.

While in Falkirk, Black was reported as having exposed himself on a number of occasions and, one time, forcibly removing a girl's underwear. At the age of 12 Black made his "first inept attempt at rape." He and two other boys took a girl their age into a field, took off her knickers and lifted her skirt but none were able to "complete the act of penetration." Instead, they touched her vagina and Black admitted that he "forced her to some degree."

After the authorities were called—and had a conference with staff at the Falkirk home—Black was sent to the higher-discipline, all-male Red House in Musselburgh. During his stay there, a male staff member regularly sexually abused him and Black began to solidify his association of sex with dominance and submission.

While in school he developed interests in both swimming and football. Due to poor eyesight he was unable to become a footballer;

however, he was well suited as a lifeguard as he was an excellent swimmer. Further, the sight of young girls in swimsuits fueled his pedophilic fantasies. In fact, 20 years later, when Caroline Hogg was abducted and murdered, her house was en route between the two swimming pools where Black worked as a teenager.

In 1962, when Black was 15, he left the children's home and procured a job as a delivery boy for a butcher. He rented a room in a boys' home in Greenock, near Glasgow, and during this time he admitted to having molested as many as 40 girls while doing his delivery rounds. He claims that when he made a delivery if a young girl was home alone he would sit down and talk to her and then try to touch her.

His first conviction was for lewd and libidinous behavior with a young girl. In 1963, at the age of 17, he approached a seven-year-old girl in a local park and asked her if she would like to accompany him to see some kittens. The naïve girl followed him into a deserted air-raid shelter. He held her by the throat until she lapsed into unconsciousness and he both masturbated over her body and sexually fondled her. She was later found wandering the streets; bleeding, crying, and confused. Black admitted that he didn't know whether she was alive or dead when he left her. Instead of lewd and libidinous behavior, Black should have been charged with and tried for attempted murder. Prior to his 25 June court date, a psychiatric evaluation concluded that this incident was an isolated one and that Black did not need any further treatment.

Black then left Greenock and returned to Grangemouth to start over. After securing employment with a builders' company and renting a room, he finally met his first real girlfriend, Pamela Hodgson. After a physical relationship he fell in love and proposed; however, she broke off the engagement not long after. He was devastated.

In 1966, Black's inappropriate sexual desires resurfaced when he repeatedly molested his landlords' nine-year old granddaughter. While the girl reported it, no charges were filed but Black was asked to leave.

Black returned to his childhood home of Kinlochleven and took a room with a couple who had a seven-year old daughter. Again, he molested the young girl; however, this time the incident was reported and he pled guilty to three counts of indecent assault and was sentenced to a year at Polmont Borstal that was known for rehabilitating the worst of the juvenile criminals. Whereas Black had no problem reiterating all of the aspects of his life and crimes, he has never discussed his time at Borstal, thus leading many to speculate that he was abused during his sentence.

Six months after he was released, Black moved to London and his discovery in child pornography quelled his immediate desire to prey upon young girls. He had discovered that magazines such as *Teenage Sex* and *Lollitots* were clandestinely available, particularly in other countries where pornography laws were less strict such as the Netherlands and he traveled to Amsterdam on several occasions. In fact, when police searched his home after the murders they found over 100 magazines and 50 videotapes depicting child pornography; in addition to Black's own discrete photographs of girls between the ages of eight and 12 he had taken which he kept with his child pornography in a locked suitcase.

Between 1968 and 1970 he held various odd jobs including working as a swimming pool attendant. While here he would oftentimes go underneath the pool, remove the lights, and watch young girls swim. One girl reported that Black had touched her inappropriately and, while no charges were filed, he was fired.

While in London, Black spent considerable time playing darts in pubs—particularly the Three Crowns Pub in Stamford Hill—and became a decent player and a well-known face on the amateur circuit. Many recall Black as a loner who preferred to drink alone irritate others, particularly ladies. During this time Black became acquainted with a Scottish couple named Edward and Kathy Rayson who offered Black lodgings in their empty attic room, which he accepted. He was responsible, albeit reclusive, who—in spite of his poor hygiene—was a model tenant. Although Mrs. Rayson did suspect her lodger of being an avid viewer and reader of pornographic material, neither of the Rayson's thought the material was pedophilic. Black lived with them until his arrest in 1990.

In 1976, after purchasing a white Fiat Transit van, Black secured employment working as a driver for the Hoxton-based Poster Dispatch and Storage, Ltd. that specialized in delivering posters—primarily of music stars—and billboard advertisements. Black would work for PDS for ten years until he was fired due to his constant minor car accidents that cost the company considerable money. Shortly after his dismissal, the company was purchased by two employees who rehired Black because even though he continued to get into accidents, he was a hard worker and was happy to cover for his coworkers by taking the longer runs others didn't care for as they interfered with family commitments. Disturbingly, Black kept a variety of masturbatory tools and girls' clothing which he would don and reenact fantasies in his head; particularly replaying the incident with the seven-year-old girl he had left for dead. When Black committed his first murder it seemed to him like the perfectly natural progression from the fantasy he replayed so frequently.

During his employment, Black became thoroughly familiar with many of London's streets, particularly its minor ones, which would enable him to easily abduct young girls and dump their bodies far from their home without witnesses.

Also during this period, Black changed his appearance multiple time; from shaving his head, growing and/or shaving a beard, and wearing a multitude of different glasses.

The Crimes

Jennifer Cardy, 9

Jennifer Cardy was abducted, sexually assaulted, and murdered on 12 August 1981; a mere two weeks after her ninth birthday. The young girl was last seen by her mother at 1:40 p.m. when she left her house in the County Antrim village of Ballinderry to ride her bicycle to her friend Louise Major's house. When Cardy didn't return home her family telephoned Major's parents where they were informed that their daughter had never even shown up at their house. Cardy's parents called the police and a search for the missing girl was immediately implemented.

Cardy's bicycle—covered with leaves and branches—was discovered an hour later less than one mile from her home. The kickstand of the bicycle was downwards which suggested that, perhaps, Cardy had stopped to talk to someone—likely her abductor—however, there were no witnesses.

Six days after Cardy's disappearance, two hunters found her body in a dam located close to a dual carriageway in Hillsborough, just 15 miles from her home. Her body displayed evident signs of sexual assault and the autopsy concluded that she had died of drowning that was most likely accompanied by ligature strangulation.

Susan Maxwell, 11

On 20 July 1982, 11-year-old Susan Maxwell from Cornhill on Tweed on the English/Scottish border left her home on her bicycle to play tennis in Coldstream. The two-mile route ensured that Maxwell would know most everyone she passed on the way and it was an area where people looked out for each other, especially the children. A number of local witnesses remembered seeing her until she crossed the bridge spanning the River Tweed.

Maxwell's mother Elizabeth reported her daughter missing after she had driven to the tennis courts to pick her up. One of her daughter's friends said that the two girls parted company outside of the Coldstream police station to walk home their separate ways.

The next day a full-scale search began, involving police and search dogs from both sides of the border. At the height of this search, over 300 officers were assigned full time to locate the young girl with activities including canvasing houses in the area and thorough searching every property within the two towns; over 80 square miles of terrain.

While there were no witnesses to the actual abduction, several people described a white van in the area.

An autopsy concluded that Maxwell had died shortly after her abduction; however, the exact date and time of death remains unknown. Maxwell remained in Black's van, whether alive or dead, for 24 hours as his delivery schedule took him into Edinburgh, Dundee, and Glasgow, where he is known to have made his final scheduled delivery at around midnight. The following day, Black returned from Glasgow to London, and discarded Maxwell's body in a copse near the A518 road near Uttoxeter, Staffordshire; 264 miles from where she was abducted.

On 12 August, Maxwell's body was found by Arthur Meadows, a lorry driver, in a ditch near the A518 road at Loxley, near Uttoxeter, in the Midlands; 250 miles from where Maxwell had been abducted. Her body was fully clothed except for her underwear and shoes and her body had been covered with undergrowth. Due to the advanced state of decomposition, she was identified by dental records. The exact date, time, and cause of death could not be determined. What was known, however, was that Maxwell had been bound, her mouth had been gagged with sticking plaster, and her underwear had been removed and neatly folded beneath her head; thus indicating that she had likely been sexually assaulted before her murder; however, the state of the body precluded knowing for sure what, exactly, happened.

Caroline Hogg, 5

Nearly a year later, five-year-Caroline Hogg became Black's youngest known victim. She disappeared while playing in a park near her Beach Lane home in Portobello—a suburb of Edinburgh—in the early evening of 8 July 1983 after begging her mother Annette for "just five more minutes" of playtime. When Hogg had not come home by

7:15 p.m. her parents and brother looked for her. A young boy around Hogg's age said that he had seen her in the company of a man on the nearby promenade, which her mother and brother frantically searched to no avail. Her mother then called the police and reported her young daughter missing.

An intensive search was undertaken which, at that time, was the largest ever in Scottish history. 2,000 local volunteers and 50 members of the infantry regiment Royal Scots Fusiliers searched all over Portobello and neighboring areas; all the way to Edinburgh. The search also attracted considerable local and national media coverage. In fact, by 10 July, the young girl's disappearance was headline news across the entire United Kingdom. Police interviewed the nine known pedophiles who were in Portobello on the night Hogg disappeared but they were all cleared.

Several eyewitnesses had seen an dirty looking, "bald man who wore glasses" watching Hogg as she played before following her to a nearby fairground named Fun City. 14-year-old Jennifer Booth saw Hogg sitting on a bench with this strange man. Booth heard Hogg reply, "Yes please," to some question posed by the man and assumed that they were father and daughter as they walked toward the fairground while holding hands. At Fun City, the man paid 15 pence for Caroline to ride the children's carousel as he watched her. Afterward, she left the fairground in his company. One child witness stated that she had seemed frightened

Not unlike his other victims, Hogg remained in Black's van for at least 24 hours and her exact date, time, and cause of death remains unknown. Black's schedule showed a poster delivery to Glasgow several hours after Hogg's disappearance and he refueled his vehicle in Carlisle in the wee hours of the following morning.

Hogg's naked body was found on 18 July in a ditch off the A444 road between Northampton to Coventry and close to the M1 motorway in Twycross, Leicestershire; 301 miles from where she had been abducted and a mere 24 miles from where Maxwell's body was discovered the previous year.

Due to advanced decomposition, Hogg was identified by her hair band and locket. The exact cause of death was undetermined; however, the entomologist who examined the body asserted that the body could not have been dumped prior to 12 July, thus suggesting that Black may have disposed of her body while making a delivery to Bedworth on the same date. That she was found completely naked also strongly suggested that her murder was sexual.

The following March, a televised reconstruction of Hogg's abduction was broadcast nationally with the hopes of producing further eyewitnesses. Additionally, all parking tickets issued in Edinburgh were examined, tourists as far as Australia were asked to send in rolls of camera and cine film they had taken in Portobello, police sat for weeks by the A444 taking down registration numbers of all vehicles that passed, and investigators searched the homes of all men identified as having been on the promenade that night for "immoral purposes." After the broadcast, Hogg's parents appealed to the public for any anonymous tips to help them find who killed their daughter. Her father said, "You think it can never happen to you, but it has proven time and time again that it can, and it could again if this man isn't caught in the near future."

Sarah Harper, 10

Three years later, ten-year-old Sarah Harper disappeared from Morley, Leeds, at approximately 7:50 p.m. on 26 March 1986, after she left her home on an errand to purchase a loaf of bread from a local market, the K&M, a mere 100 yards from her home. The shop's owner, Mrs. Champaneri confirmed that the girl did, in fact, purchase a loaf of bread and two packages of crisps at approximately 7:55 p.m. and left at 8:05 p.m. She also stated that a balding man entered her store moments later and left when Harper left.

Harper was last seen by two girls walking into an alley leading towards her Brunswick Place home; a shortcut that locals used. When she had not returned by 8:20 p.m., her mother, Jackie, and sister, Claire, briefly searched the surrounding streets before reporting the young girl missing to West Yorkshire Police at approximately 9:00 p.m. Police—as in the other cases—immediately launched an extensive search for the child with over 100 police officers being assigned full-time to look for the young girl. This search involved house-to-house canvases across Morley; the search of over 3,000 properties; distribution of over 10,000 flyers; and the taking of 1,400 witness statements. Additionally, another 200 local volunteers helped search surrounding areas including the search of a reservoir in nearby Tingley by underwater units.

West Yorkshire Police confirmed that a white Transit van had been seen in the area where Harper had been abducted while two suspicious men had been seen in the vicinity near where Harper walked to the store. One of them was a stocky, balding man. Believing that Harper had likely been abducted the police sent a telex to all forces nationwide requesting that they search the areas where other child murder victims had been found.

At a 3 April press conference, Harper's mother Jackie told journalists that she believed her daughter was dead but that the worst thing was not knowing. Appealing to the abductor, Jackie said, "I just want her back, even if she's dead. If someone would just pick up the phone and tell us where the body is." Afterward, Jackie fainted.

On 19 April, while walking his dog, a man named David Moult found Sarah's naked body, gagged and bound, floating in the River Trent near Nottingham, nearly seventy miles from where she was kidnapped.

An autopsy revealed that while the cause of death was drowning, she sustained injuries to her head and neck which likely rendered her unconscious before she was thrown into the water. In addition to being beaten, the evidence demonstrated that Harper had been the victim of a violent and sustained sexual assault—including being sodomized—prior to being tossed into the river. The pathologist described these pre-mortem injuries as "simply terrible." The young victim's father, Terry, Jackie's ex-husband, had to identify his daughter's body and stated that "it was worse than I ever dreamed of."

Investigation and Arrest

By the spring of 1983, whereas many detectives assigned to the inquiry into Maxwell's murder were assigned elsewhere, several detectives did, in fact, remain on the case. When Hogg's body was found in July 1983, Detective Chief Superintendent of Staffordshire Police Dennis Boden held an emergency meeting with senior Staffordshire and Leicestershire detectives to explore the possibility that the same person was responsible for both murders.

Cardy's murder would not be formally linked to the other cases until 2009.

Due to the distance between where the victims were abducted and subsequently found, police suspected that the same person was responsible and that he worked in an occupation that required extensive travel across the United Kingdom, such as a lorry or van driver, or some type of sales representative. Additionally, that both victims were bound and likely subjected to sexual assault—and were clad in white ankle socks when they disappeared—it was presumed that this triggered some sort of fetish response by the perpetrator. It was also decided that due to the circumstantial and geographical nature of the crimes that the perpetrator was likely an opportunist.

Further, since both Maxwell and Hogg were abducted on a Friday, the perpetrator most likely had some sort of delivery or production schedule. After discovery of the bodies, police contacted all transport firms with deliveries in Scotland and the Midlands and all drivers were questioned as to their whereabouts on the dates of the abductions; however, this tactic failed to uncover any potential leads.

Complete cooperation existed between police from the four separate police departments involved in the manhunt. Initially, a satellite incident room that was based in Coldstream coordinated the collective efforts for leads in the Maxwell case while additional incident rooms in Leith and Portobello coordinate the search for evidence in Hogg's case. However, within hours of the discovery of Hogg's body, there was overwhelming consensus that both cases were linked and that they should join efforts with one investigating officer to coordinate all inquiries. Assistant Chief Constable of Northumbia Police Hector Clark was appointed to lead the investigation. Clark established incident rooms in Northumberland and Leith police stations to coordinate all efforts to search for the girls' murderer.

Initially, all information related to both cases was logged with a card-filing system that initially grew to over 500,000 index cards just for the Maxwell case alone. Being familiar with the criticism levied against police during the Yorkshire Ripper case for their being overwhelmed due to the sheer volume of information filed with this type of system, Clark introduced computerized technology into the investigation. Collective use of a computerized database that everyone involved in the investigation could access would improve results. Thus, by December 1986, all of the information related to the three murders (thus far) would be entered into the HOLMES information technology system and additional information would continue to be entered so that police forces nationwide would be able to cross-check all data entered into the system. Initially, detectives looked at individuals who had been convicted of serious sexual crimes against children within the ten years prior to Maxwell's murder in 1982 be further investigated. The list of potential suspects was narrowed to 40,000; however, Black's name never arose as his only conviction was in 1967.

Eventually, this database that was based at the Child Murder Bureau in the West Yorkshire city of Bradford would expand to hold information on over 187,000 individuals; 220,000 vehicles; and 57,000 witness interviews. Much of the information in the database had been obtained through three confidential hotlines established in 1984 by the inquiry team which eventually enabled police to solve numerous other, unrelated crimes, including child abuse offenses.

Several days after Harper's abduction and murder, a witness contacted West Yorkshire Police to inform authorities that on 26 March, at approximately 9:15 p.m., he had seen a white van parked close to the River Soar. A stocky, balding man was standing by the passenger door. Because the River Soar is a tributary to the River Trent and that the vehicle's and man's descriptions were similar to those given by other witnesses, investigators took this account seriously. Furthermore, Black is known to have refueled his van in the Newport Pagnell, Buckinghamshire, the following afternoon; which may suggest that he had taken Harper to the village of Ratcliffe on Soar and had discarded her body in the river either in the evening of the day she was abducted or in the early hours the following morning. Because Harper's abductor likely traveled on the M1 motorway before disposing of her body, investigators from both West Yorkshire and Nottinghamshire Police Departments questioned motorists and staff at all service stations along the M1 motorway between Woolley and Trowell as to whether they might have seen anything unusual on the 26th or 27th of March. Staff at one service station did, in fact, remember a white Transit van that had "seemed out of place" on the evening of 26 March; however, they could not provide a clear description of the driver.

Clark initially did not believe that Harper's murder was connected to Maxwell's and Hogg's due to several dissimilarities; however, in retrospect there were glaring and perhaps more telling similarities. All of the victims were young girls skillfully abducted from public places for sexual purposes and they were driven south and murdered. Further, the three bodies were found within 26 miles of each other in a triangular area known as the Midlands Triangle. Even though Harper's sexual assault appeared to be more vicious than the other two, experts assert that serial killers frequently increase their violence as the murderer gains more confidence and requires more brutality to achieve and maintain arousal. Eight months after Harper was found, Her Majesty's Inspector of Constabulary determined that all three murders were, in fact, linked and that one database be established. Entering all information into a single database took three years and was completed in July 1990.

In 1986, investigators formally requested assistance from the FBI to create a profile of their perpetrator which was completed in January 1988. This profile described the killer as a 30- to 40-year-old white male, likely a loner, who would likely be unkempt in appearance and had received less than 12 years of formal education. He probably lived alone, rented his home, and was in a middle-class neighborhood. Additionally, the profile surmised that the murderer's motives were purely sexual and that he likely had a fixation or obsession with child pornography. Profilers also hypothesized that the killer retained souvenirs from his victims and likely engaged in necrophilia with his victims' bodies shortly after their deaths.

Black was arrested on 14 July 1990, near Stow, Scotland, after snatching six-year-old Mandy Wilson off of the street and bundling her into his van. An alert neighbor, 53-year-old retired postmaster David Herkes, took down the van's registration number and called the police. After a chase, Black was apprehended. The victim was actually the daughter of one of the police officers on the scene and he discovered his daughter in the back of the van, bound and gagged, and stuffed into a sleeping bag. Prior to tying her up, Black had sexually assaulted her. Black was charged with plagium (kidnapping).

When Black's residence was searched, investigators discovered a large collection of child pornography.

Trial and Sentencing

In August 1990, Black was tried and convicted of kidnapping Wilson and given a life sentence. The sentence was based, largely, upon psychiatrists' testimony that Black would continue to pose a great threat to young girls.

Black was still the prime suspect in the murders of Susan Maxwell, Caroline Hogg, and Sarah Harper. Clark decided to interview Black as he was already serving a life sentence for the Wilson kidnapping and Clark mentioned that when he first saw him his gut feeling was that Black was his man. However, instinct and a gut feeling are not good enough for procuring a guilty conviction in a court of law. Black spoke candidly about his prior convictions, about his short relationship with his fiancée, about the sexual abuse he had endured as a child, about his fantasy life, and about his masturbatory practices. When asked specific questions about the three murders he fell silent.

A check of Black's gas receipts and delivery schedules placed him in the vicinity of each girl's abduction and he was charged with all three murders, as well as the attempted kidnapping of a 15-year-old girl who had escaped from the man who tried to drag her into his van in 1988. In this case, on 28 April 1988, 15-year-old Teresa Thornhill had been walking home from the park where she had met friends when Thornhill noticed a blue van stopped ahead. When the driver asked her for help and she denied, he had grabbed her from behind and was taking her to his van. She recalled that he was sweaty and stinky and was able to grab his testicles while screaming. Her friend Andrew, hearing her screams, came to help his friend and chase the assailant away.

Black's murder trial began on 13 April 1994 in front of Judge William MacPherson. Black pled not guilty to the ten charges levied against him which included murder, kidnapping, and preventing the lawful burial of a body. Despite his denial of any guilt, the prosecution was able to place him at each scene and to demonstrate similarities between the three murders and the prior kidnapping for which he had already been convicted and sentenced. His trial lasted five weeks.

On 19 May, the jury found Black guilty of all charges and he was sentenced to life imprisonment with a minimum of 35 years for each charge, to be served concurrently; thus rendering him 82 years old before being eligible for parole—if he were still alive at that time.

On 15 December, Black had been served a formal summons charging him with the murder and sexual assault of Jennifer Cardy and his second murder trial began at Armagh Crown Court on 22 September 2011 before Judge Ronald Weatherup. As he did regarding his other three victims, Black pled not guilty.

Evidence such as gas receipts and delivery schedules demonstrated that Black was in the area at the time Cardy disappeared. This second trial lasted six weeks and on 27 October 2011 he was found guilty of abducting, murdering, and sexually assaulting Cardy. He was given another life sentence.

Aftermath

Black suffered a fatal heart attack while incarcerated at HMP Maghaberry on 12 January 2016, just weeks before he was to be charged with the murder of 13-year-old Genette Tate who had disappeared while delivering newspapers on 19 August 1978 in Aylesbeare, Devon, England.

Senior detectives believe that Black was responsible for eight deaths, in addition to the Tate case; however, 12 other child murders committed across the UK, Ireland, and continental Europe between 1969 and 1987 have also been linked to Black. These include: April Fabb, 13, 8 April 1969, UK; Christine Markham, 9, 21 May 1973, UK; Suzanne Lawrence, 14, 22 July 1979, UK; Patricia Morris, 14, 16 June 1980, UK; Pamela Hastie, 16, 4 November 1981, UK; Mary Boyle, 6, 18 March 1977, Ireland; Silke Garben, 10, 20 June 1985, Germany; Cheryl Morriën, 7, 5 August 1986, Netherlands; Virginie Delmas, 10, 5 May 1987, France; Hemma Devy-Greedharry, 10, 30 May 1987, France; Perrine Vigneron, 7, 3 June 1987, France; and Sabine Dumont, 9, 27 June 1987, France. In all of these cases, Black is known to have been in the area or a white van with a driver who resembled Black was seen.

Prior to his death, Black never admitted culpability in any of the murders for which he was convicted and suspected.

His body was cremated on 29 January and his ashes were discarded at sea.

SICKO JOSEPH DUNCAN

144

Joseph E. Duncan III

Joseph E. Duncan III is a convicted serial killer, serial rapist, pedophile, stalker, abductor, and sex offender who is currently on death row in Terre Haute, Indiana awaiting his execution date. He was born and raised in Tacoma, Washington on February 25, 1963.

It did not take long for Joseph Duncan to take a wrong direction in life. Supposedly his first sexual encounter was at the age of eight years old with two of his sisters. Four years after that, at the age of twelve, he then sexually assaulted a five-year-old boy. Although this was something he later told a therapist, nothing was confirmed and no chargers were filed. At the tender age of fifteen, he stole a car and led police on a high-speed chase. He ended up crashing into a roadbloc and fled from the vehicle. At the age of sixteen, he kidnapped and forced a fourteen-year-old boy to perform oral sex before raping him (some sources assert that there was another nine year old boy who he raped at gunpoint at some point in time).

He was ultimately charged, pleading guilty to first-degree rape with a firearm and was given a twenty-year sentence. However, it was after these two incidents that he was sentenced to a number of months at Dyslin's Boys Ranch in Tacoma, Washington, a treatment center. While recovering and receiving therapy at the ranch, he told one of his therapists that he had already raped thirteen boys. His modus operandi was to bind them up and repeatedly torture them with sexual assaults.

In 1980, by the time he was seventeen years old he was sentenced to twenty years behind bars for raping a fourteen-year-old boy, again at gunpoint. He broke into a neighbor's house, stole a gun and then forced the young boy into a nearby wooded area with threats of using the gun on him. He sexually assaulted the boy twice before beating him and burning him with cigarettes. Duncan would let the boy go and was later charged with first-degree rape, first-degree burglary and third-degree statutory rape.

While in prison for this rape he was forced to take part in a Sexual Offender Program at Western State Hospital. However, after just under two years in this program his therapist concluded that the therapy was not something that would be helpful to Duncan. He was not willing to adhere to the rules or facility staff; therefore, he was sent back to the state penitentiary where he would serve the rest of his prison sentence. However, some reports state that he was released because he was sneaking out and peeping on other women.

Throughout his sentence he had numerous reviews for protective custody, issues with other inmates, and sexual misconduct. In 1985, he was able to take a job as a teacher's aide at the prison. Unfortunately, he took advantage of that job when he was found sneaking off peeping into homes and masturbating. This particular progress review even mentions that future paroles should bar him from contact with minors. In April of 1988, he took a new job at the prison as a tool crib attendant. By August of that year he was sentenced to ten days of segregation for having a VCR and two x-rated movies in his room. At numerous times throughout his stay in prison from 1988 to 1994 he was put into segregation or was under review for infractions related to sexual misconduct. Many times those who reviewed him said that he needed close supervision and specialized treatment.

He was paroled fourteen years later in 1994 with the understanding that he would have absolutely no contact with children. He went to a halfway house (Interaction Transition House) to try and straighten up his life. He did hold a job as a telemarketer for a little while but would later break parole in 1996 after being caught with marijuana and a firearm. Once again, he was back in jail for thirty days. Joseph Duncan would later have a parole revocation hearing to determine whether he should stay in jail or be released. Dr. Wacksman testified on his behalf, but the board denied his request. Duncan went back to prison until July of 2000. Upon his release he traveled up to Washington for a visit with his mother and then to Fargo, North Dakota for a visit with Dr. Wacksman.

What he did during the few years between 2000 until the 2005 murders and kidnapping of Mark McKenzie and the Groene's is not completely known and probably never will be. Although, he did confessed to some additional crimes while in jail for the 2005 murders of Mark McKenzie and the Groene's, there are probably several more that investigators will never know about. The 2005 murders and kidnapping as well as several other crimes are outlined below.

Sammiejo White and Carmen Cubias

After Joseph Duncan's thirty days in jail he was staying a few blocks from a motel that Sammiejo White and Carmen Cubias were staying. Both the eleven year old, Sammiejo, and nine year old, Carmen, went missing from the motel on July 6, 1996. The two sisters were leaving the motel late in the evening to go get cigarettes for their older brother.

They never returned.

It was not uncommon for these children to be out so late. In fact, there were several other siblings in this household and they were all known in the neighborhood.

Police never knew if the girls ran away or were victims of a crime. However, their bodies were found two years later on February 10, 1998 in Bothell, Washington. It was determined that they were probably killed shortly after being kidnapped. The case was denoted a cold case for years until August of 2005 when Joseph Duncan provided police with details of what happened to the two girls in 1996. Although he never actually confessed, he did give enough specific details of what happened to the girls that made for an easy confession. An eyewitness later confirmed that she saw Joseph Duncan and a girl that looked like Carmen Cubias at a grocery store. The girl seemed frightened from what the witness said. This was one of Duncan's signature moves (keeping victims alive for a period of time). The details from each of his cases are very similar making it easier to link past cases and crimes to Duncan.

Anthony Martinez

Joseph Duncan was also implicated in a 1997 case involving a ten-year-old boy in California. On April 4, 1997 an unknown man approached Anthony Martinez at his home in Beaumont, California. He and some of his friends were playing football in his front yard when the man asked for help finding his cat. All of the boys refused his help the strange man, but the man became enraged and grabbed one of the boys. He used a knife to scare the boy and the other kids. He put the child who was later identified as Anthony Martinez in his vehicle and fled the scene.

On April 19, 2005 Anthony Martinez's body was found in Indio naked and bound. An autopsy revealed that Anthony had been brutally sexually assaulted. Although there was duct tape used to bind Anthony and a partial fingerprint from that tape, the case did go cold. It was not until after the 2005 Idaho murder that Joseph Duncan was tied to the Martinez case. Once the Federal Bureau of Investigations (FBI) started tying similarities together, it become obvious that Joseph Duncan was involved. Authorities tested his fingerprints against the one found on the tape and it was a confirmed match.

After the 2005 kidnapping and murders of the Groene and McKenzie family, Joseph Duncan did confess to the murder of Anthony Martinez; therefore, in April of 2011 Duncan plead guilty to the murder of Antony Martinez and received two consecutive life sentences for his death.

Duncan was then sentenced to life in prison in 2011 for the murder of Anthony Martinez.

2005 Idaho Murders

The 2005 killing and kidnapping spree of Joseph Duncan began because of his bond release from a Minnesota jail. First, it is important to note that he was in jail because of the suspected molestation of two boys. In March of 2005, he was charged with the July 3, 2004 molestation of two boys at a playground in Detroit Lakes, Minnesota. His bond was for about $15,000 and after being released from jail he skipped his bond. He began making plans to leave the state immediately.

He was able to convince a businessman, Joe Crary, to pay his $15,000 bond (with a personal check). Apparently they had a romantic relationship and Joseph Duncan did an outstanding job of making it seem like he was a misunderstood man with the discipline to turn his life around. Little did Joe Crary know what was coming next would be one of the worst crimes in Idaho history.

Joseph Duncan meticulously planned his crime, stopping to pick up tools at a Walmart. He bought night vision goggles, a video camera, a shotgun, shells, and a claw hammer. After about two weeks, he decided it was time to leave the state of Minnesota. He rented a red Jeep Grand Cherokee in St. Paul, Minnesota and traveled out of state. He went through Missouri then entered Idaho with plans to go on a killing rampage.

Duncan stole license places off of another vehicle and placed them on the red Jeep Cherokee to avoid detection and capture. He knew that at some point the vehicle he rented would be reported as stolen. He drove up Interstate 90 towards Coeur d'Alene, Idaho. He made landfall there roughly five weeks after his hearing for sexually assaulting a six-year-old boy. Authorities do not know exactly why he stopped in Coeur d'Alene, Idaho, possibly for gas or food, but he did. He located the Groene and McKenzie home in a secluded area, not far off the frontage road.

Duncan saw Shasta Groene (eight years old) and her brother, Dylan (nine years old), playing in the front yard of the house. It was the kind of neighborhood where people felt confident in letting thier children play outside at will. Children played at the park, rode their bikes and came and went from house to house without a care in the world. A world that didn't have the likes of Joseph Duncan until now.

The Groene and McKenzie home was one of the first houses you see when one enters the neighborhood, but also very secluded with trees. The house was off the frontage road a ways, but positioned in a way that it was the first one available in case of an emergency. Many strangers had stopped by before if there was a problem and they needed help. The Groene and McKenzie family never turned anyone away. They were always willing to help someone in needed.

It is believed that Joseph Duncan was intrigued by the children and the ease of the community that this felt like the right time and the right family to attack. He used a few days to survey the family and perform reconnaissance prior to confronting them. May 15th, 2005 was the last time anyone saw Mark McKenzie, Brenda Groene and Slade Groene alive. The family had been to a large barbeque with other neighbors that evening before heading home.

Authorities were alerted on Monday, May 16, 2005, when a neighbor went by the residence to pay Slade for mowing his grass the day before. The neighbor said that the house was very quiet, there were no lights on in the house, but both vehicles were home with car doors left open. It seemed odd and it was appropriate that authorities check it out. It is also important to note that the same neighbor had seen a white pick up at the house earlier in the day. Apparently that neighbor was the one that called authorities to report the suspicious activity earlier in the day

The Kootenai County Sheriff's Department sent deputies to check out the house and check on the family. After surveying the outside of the house, deputies decided to gain access to the house to check on the wellness of the homeowners.

Upon entering the house from the backyard, they found two bodies in the kitchen area that were duct taped and zip tied. Both had been brutally killed either by blunt force trauma to the head or a gunshot wound. One was a male and the other was a female. Deputies also found an additional victim in the living room, also bound by duct tape and zip tied. Again, the third victim had blunt force trauma to the head or a gunshot wound. After investigating the rest of the house, it was determined that the three victims were Mark McKenzie, his girlfriend Brenda Groene, and her son, thirteen year-old Slade Groene. Brenda's younger children, Shasta Groene (eight years old) and Dylan Groene (nine years old), were nowhere to be found.

At this point, the case then turned to the two missing children. Search teams gathered to cover terrain around the Groene and McKenzie home and Lake Coeur d'Alene. The search team included deputies with trained search dogs, helicopters, volunteers on foot, as well as the Federal Bureau of Investigation (FBI). An Amber Alert was issued with pictures and descriptions to ensure as many people as possible knew about the two missing children. Authorities also set up an emergency tip line that allowed citizens to call in tips if they had any information about the two missing children. Within the first twelve hours, the police had over 150 calls. Volunteers helped take calls and sift through the information to determine what might be a valuable lead or not. Some tips included information about where the children's favorite play spots were, possible sightings, etc. Unfortunately, the tips did not generate many useful leads and most did not pan out. This case quickly became the largest in Kootenai County history and even generated an FBI reward of $100,000. However, the case was not generating any traction. The case was growing cold every day. America's Most Wanted even ran a special on May 21, 2005 to help generate new leads to find the children. Nine new tips came in, but none of them panned out either.

However, two days prior to the America's Most Wanted TV special, the children's biological father gave a heartfelt plea to release his children. During that time frame, a sporting goods store own in Bonners Ferry, Idaho called in to the police department with a huge tip. He told deputies that a man with two children fitting Shasta and Dylan's descriptions came into the store asking for directions to Montana. He said that they left in a white van with Washington state license plates. Unfortunately, even after notifying Idaho State Police there were no signs of the van or the children.

During this time, investigators were still trying to determine the cause of the deaths of Brenda, Mark and Slade. Several different scenarios were being suggested for motive, especially after toxicology results determined that both Brenda and Mark had THC and methamphetamines in their system at the time of their death. First, investigators tried to determine if it was one person or more that killed the family. Since they were bound, investigators thought there may have been more than one person involved. Some ideas included a drug deal gone bad, gang killings, or something similar. The motive for the killings and the kidnappings were dumbfounding to investigators.

Time was slipping away from authorities making this investigation harder and harder on everyone involved. However, on July 2nd at 1:30 in the morning the same red Jeep Cherokee that Joseph Duncan had rented just after his release from jail showed up at a local Denny's in Coeur d'Alene. A middle aged man and a little girl matching the description of Shasta walked into the restaurant together. Two men outside the restaurant and a waitress inside the restaurant recognized little Shasta. They quietly notified the manager of the Denny's who called 911. Three police cars showed up about ten minutes after the middle-aged man and little Shasta arrived at Denny's.

Joseph Duncan was arrested and Shasta was rescued. Unfortunately, Dylan was not found in the Jeep Cherokee.

After Shasta was rescued, police were able to put a better timeline together. Joseph Duncan broke into the Groene and McKenzie home in the middle of the night on July 5, 2005. Shasta's mother, Brenda, woke up her and carried her into the living room where she encountered Joseph Duncan. Duncan took Shasta and Dylan to a white truck outside. He placed them into the truck where they did not witness the brutal murders of Mark, Brenda and Slade. After Duncan murdered the rest of the family, he took Shasta and Dylan to a remote location where the Jeep Cherokee was hidden. He used a white truck to transport the kids to the Jeep Cherokee. He then moved the children to the other vehicle and took off for Montana. The three of them stayed in two separate campsites in Montana for six weeks where Joseph Duncan repeatedly raped and sexually abused both Shasta and her brother, Dylan.

Shasta told investigators that Duncan told her in vivid detail how he killed her family and how he watched them for several days prior to breaking into their home. He also told her the he sexually assaulted her other brother Slade. She was able to give enough details about their campsite that investigators were also able to locate the place where Duncan kept them, which ultimately led to the discovery of Dylan's remains.

Joseph Duncan was originally charged with two counts of first-degree kidnapping in Idaho, which warrants death, or life in prison. With evidence linking him to the Groene and McKenzie murders, he was also charged with three counts of first-degree murder, which means that Joseph Duncan would serve three consecutive life sentences. Although after recovering Dylan's body it was determined the little boy was shot to death and burned to cover up evidence. With this discovery, an additional charge of murder was added. At this point, Duncan also chooses to waive his right to appeal the death sentences.

Joseph Duncan is currently on death row awaiting his execution date for these murders.

Dr. Richard Wacksman

Dr. Richard Wacksman testified on behalf of Joseph Duncan during his parole violation hearing in 1997. He told the court that Duncan was no longer a harm or danger to society and that he was a reformed citizen. He also told the court that Joseph Duncan could come live with him while he got back on his feet. Evidentially, Dr. Wacksman had helped quite a few felons get back on their feet in the past. The court clearly did not believe Duncan was ready for society yet and sent him back to prison for three more years until 2000. Then on July 21, 2000, Duncan moved to Fargo, North Dakota. Dr. Wacksman helped Duncan out by giving him money, a place to stay, a car, and even money for tuition to North Dakota State University.

Apparently, the two had a romantic relationship, even though Dr. Wacksman was married with children. The two met in the mid-90's at a gay bar in San Francisco. Eventually Dr. Wacksman moved to Florida, which Duncan did visit quite often for scuba diving trips. The two men stayed in heavy contact until Dr. Wacksman realized that Joseph Duncan was manipulating him every step of the way.

Other Potential Victims

Other possible victims of Joseph Duncan include Steven Earl Kraft Jr., Russell Turcotte, Leanne "Beaner" Warner, Justin Phillip Edwards and other molestation victims.

Steven Earl Kraft, Jr., a twelve year-old boy took his two dogs out for an evening walk in Benton Harbor, Michigan on February 15, 2001. He was last seen leaving around 7:00 pm with both dogs, but only one dog came back. That dog led his parents to a local pond, but there was nothing there to reflect that Steven Kraft, Jr. had been there. Although the other dog, a puppy, was later found near a creek. To this date, the case still remains unsolved and is a cold case, but it is suspected that Joseph Duncan is somehow involved in the kidnapping and possible murder of this young teen.

Russell Turcotte, a nineteen year-old boy was last heard from by his mother. He contacted her for money, needing a bus ticket home. Last seen in Grand Folks, North Dakota on July 12, 2002 after a weekend with friends. His remains were found at Devils Lake about ninety miles east of the truck stop. Surveillance cameras at the truck stop have both Russel Turcotte and Joseph Duncan at the truck stop within hours of each other. The probable story is that Duncan picked up a hitch hiking Russell Turcotte to or from the truck strop. Duncan most likely took Russell to a remote location, raped him and then killed him just like his other signature cases. Russell's body was not found until November of 2002. One of the biggest reasons that Joseph Duncan is a suspect in this case, besides being seen at the truck stop, is the fact that Russell Turcotte's head was crushed in much the same manner as Duncan's prior victims have been (Sammiejo White, Carmen Cubias, Anthony Martinez, Mark McKenzie and Slade Groene). The similarities in the cases are too coincidental not to suspect Joseph Duncan as a possibility.

Leanne "Beaner" Warner was last seen on June 14, 2003. Beaner was a nickname her grandfather affectionately gave her. She was only five years old at the time she went missing. Beaner headed over to a friend's house that evening, but the family was out at the time of her arrival. Two eyewitness neighbors stated they did see little Beaner around 5:00 pm. When Beaner did not show back up from her friend's house her parents Chris and Kaelin Warner became worried. They finally contacted police around 9:00 pm after the parents went looking themselves. The family lived in a small town of Chisholm, Minnesota. The town is home to roughly 5,000 people and was considered a safe community. The police initially thought maybe she got lost; there were no leads that made them think an abduction had occurred. Although search dogs did find her scent at Longyear Lake as well as her footprints, no other evidence was uncovered. She was also at the lake earlier in the day with her mother, so it was hard to determine if this was relevant or not. However, it is important to note that Joseph Duncan would make frequent trips to this area for scuba diving trips. On this particular day he went skydiving with friends near West Fargo, North Dakota where he has pictures and videos that puts him close to the location. In Duncan's video, he discusses his scuba diving trip that he had taken in the Chisholm area within a few days of Beaner's disappearance. The video also includes tons of footage of children running and playing in an airport. A little random for someone to have children they do not know on their video. In his blog he also talks about this crime in detail. Unfortunately, Beaner's case is still cold and he has never confessed to her crime. He is still a prime suspect.

Justin Phillip Harris was last seen at his group home in Casper, Wyoming. The morning that the staff found him missing his bed was made so that it looked like someone was still sleeping in it. It is not likely that Justin could do this because he was mentally disabled with the mind of a six year old. There is nothing that ties Duncan to this disappearance, but his blog states that he went skiing over that weekend alone. It is believed that he is involved somehow.

Joseph Duncan is also suspected in numerous other molestations throughout his years out of prison.

Conclusion

Joseph E. Duncan III is a sick individual that should have been locked away for life many, many, years ago. He has repeatedly committed crimes that make it obvious he is not fit for society and a nuisance to everyone he comes into contact with. He is a serial killer and sex offender that is a danger to society. The horrendous acts he has committed are beyond comprehension and unthinkable to even those in law enforcement.

Currently, his attorneys continue to file appeals on his behalf to overturn his death sentences (against his will by the way). The latest attempt was in March of 2015 with his attorneys fighting to overrule that he was mentally competent when he waived his right to appeal the 2005 murder and kidnapping of nine year old, Anthony Martinez. This has yet to be resolved, so Joseph Duncan is still on death row awaiting execution by lethal injection.

Duncan is still expressing his life and feelings on his blog "The Fifth Nail Exposed: Confessions". The site is broken down into categories: Introductions, Letters, Reflections, Inquiry, Confessions, Dreams,

Chronicles and Books. He basically details vivid memories from his childhood to specific crimes he has committed.